WORD of GOD ACROSS the AGES

Bill J. Leonard

BROADMAN PRESS
Nashville, Tennessee

To
Candyce C. Leonard
who listened and cared

4265-57
ISBN: 0-8054-6557-x

Dewey Decimal Classification: 270
Subject heading: CHURCH HISTORY
Library of Congress Catalog Card Number: 80-67780
Printed in the United States of America

Contents

Foreword

Christians like to say that theirs is a historical faith. By this they mean that while some religions recycle souls through endless ages and time leads nowhere, in their understanding God has a romance with time. God at some point started a story by creating a world and peopling it with men and women who have earthly beginnings and endings. This God visits them in the sacred voice in a burning bush, leads them, chastises them, gives them new starts. When they fail, this God enters time and history in Jesus Christ, and propels into the future a community of believers until the end time.

For all these reasons, Christians have a great investment in history. They are not museum keepers, antique shop owners, custodians of antiquarian treasures, or guides to the City of the Dead. Theirs is a living Lord, and their past points to a future. The stories they tell are not told to amuse but to save, and they are not about dead tradition but, by the power of the Holy Spirit, enliveners. They draw on a history book called the Bible, but they see that book, in a way, as an unfinished one, with them in the plot. While other religions worship apart from a historical sense, the Christians do not reenact what happens in the lives of distant deities. All Christian worship remembers and builds on historical events: the Passover, the nativity, the death and resurrection of Jesus.

In all these respects, Christians are devoted to history.

Yet their devotion to history is one of the best-kept secrets in the Christian world.

Rare is the local church that tells stories about any past but its own. As if the Holy Spirit were silent and unmoving for twenty centuries, there is silence about the men and women who walked by and lived in faith and hope and love. Rare is the local church that ever sees a historical film, has a class on church history, or hears a pastor preach on the story of people between biblical times and now. A few Christian colleges let you in on the secret about the past, but church history is a quiet subject. Seminaries cram a bit of history down the throats of students who have a few compulsory courses and occasional electives as they get down to more serious business like learning how to run mimeograph machines.

Professor Bill Leonard does not think things should be left like this. He thinks that the story of men and women of the past is too exciting to be left to university professors in history departments or even to seminaries. He wants to take the story on the road, to the local churches. The way he has chosen to do this is not through a series of addresses on everything that ever happened in the past. Instead, he concentrates on a few giant and a few lesser-known figures.

The people about whom he preaches are something like templates, whose outlines we can trace and follow in determining our ways of life. They are molds into which we can fit dimensions of personality, models we can pay attention to when we make choices. This does not mean that any of the people are infallible or unflawed. They have gigantic faults, from which we can learn. Sometimes their flaws are so major that one wonders how he has the nerve to talk about them and hold them up at all. Yet, the closer one gets to their images, their need for grace, the more this strikes us: they are just like biblical people. John Wesley's pettiness in Georgia is not attractive to people who admire Wesley, but it is trivial compared to the Goliath-sized sins of a David in the Bible.

What also comes through in these lives is a sense that these people realized a gift of grace that gave them daily new starts. This is something that many sermons do not do. They offer Bible texts, doctrines, and moral injunctions, but they do not show us much of what the Christian life looks like. The Leonard sermons do. We have something to grasp in the imagination when we hear about real people.

Were these just historical lectures, they would not belong in the pulpit. The last thing the pulpit needs is more people who talk "about" God. The Christian people are starved for a message which does not just describe God but which offers God, makes God real in their lives. Leonard does not stop short and say, "Now here comes the enactment of judgment and of grace. Here I stop lecturing and want to draw you aside and start preaching." Instead, he works on the assumption that to depict these lives with his purpose in view is part of that offering of God as a living presence and a lively gift to people today.

Sermons on historical beings will never replace those rooted in biblical texts. In fact, had I my hand in advising him—and he needs precious little advice—I probably would have urged him to hook each life more deeply onto a motivating biblical text. But he chose to say that his represents one way of preaching alongside others. On other days the preacher can dig deep, deep, deep into biblical texts. What he or she finds in such texts and brings back to light will be more vivid in the minds of congregants who have heard sermon series like this one.

The book has several uses. Thanks to the last chapter, there is advice to preachers who can begin to learn how to preach on lives of Christians. I think it can serve as an introduction to Christian biography and history for people who do not care that the chapters ever were sermons and who never preach. There are references to the Baptist world which a non-Baptist like the present sinner feels outside of. But that is part of what one feels as an eavesdropper in any worship; it is not a limitation but a way of reminding us that the Word of God always comes to us in specific contexts. Leonard lets us in on his, and it only takes a moment or two to feel at home. I hope that if these sermons or chapters are attractive to Christians in general, they will not go unheard, unread, or unheeded in the Baptist house—or churches. They have come along at just the proper time for those who have ears to hear, and eyes to see.

MARTIN E. MARTY

Fairfax M. Cone Distinguished Service Professor
The University of Chicago

Introduction

Matthew's Gospel (11:2-6) contains an interesting and sometimes overlooked account of an exchange between John the Baptizer and Jesus of Nazareth. John is in prison, soon to be executed, and the outspoken prophet is, at least for the moment, entertaining second thoughts. John had baptized Jesus, proclaiming him to be the one promised by God for the deliverance of his people. He had expected great things from his insightful cousin but now he is apparently not so sure. For John is in prison, the kingdom has not come, and the Promised One has not yet made his move. Thus John sends word to Jesus: "Are you the one, or should we wait for another?"

It is a timeless inquiry of faith. For sooner or later most of those who believe, and many who do not, ask such questions. "Have we heard it correctly?" "Is it really God's word which has come to us?" "How can we be sure?" In a sense, Christian history is an account of the ways in which men and women have asked and answered those questions regarding the trustworthiness of Jesus and his word.

This book is about that search for the word of God and the ways in which it has been discovered by diverse persons in diverse times. The sermons provided here may be said to have two basic purposes. First, they suggest that the word of God is always out ahead of us. It goes beyond our preconceived expectations and our absolute assurances to work where we never expected it to work and do what we least expected it to do. It is indeed elusive and it comes to persons in inexplicable and unanticipated circumstances.

Second, in the face of the elusive quality of the word of God the church must learn humility. No single institution or believer can ever know or hear all the word at any given time. Even the most insightful believers of Christian history were limited in their interpretation of the word by their own culture, prejudices, and sins. Jesus described us all when he told a story about the Pharisee and the publican who went to the Temple to pray. One was certain that he knew the word of God, what it meant, where it could be found, and to whom it applied. He boasted arrogantly of the strength of his character and his faith. The other, a public sinner, made no such presumptions. He merely took the word to heart and called for mercy. That man discovered the reality of the word even when he was supposed to be outside its boundaries.

Throughout much of its history, the church has frequently answered questions regarding the reality of the word of God with responses similar to those two men. The individuals discussed in these sermons were sometimes Pharisees who became publicans when the word of God finally reached them. Occasionally they were publicans who became Pharisees. Whatever their circumstances, they were arrested by the elusive word of God and their struggle with that word may inform our own struggles.

These sermons were first presented at a series of ecumenical services shared by two congregations in the town of Southborough, Massachusetts, during the summer of 1974. One of those congregations, the First Community Church, is a diverse group of friends and neighbors from varied denominational traditions who choose not to go outside their community for worship and ministry. I served as pastor of the church from 1971 to 1975 and during those years was introduced to the benefits and struggles of a small nondenominational fellowship. When we united with the Pilgrim Church (UCC) for summer services and added a wayward Episcopalian or two, the congregation truly reflected the broad nature of Christ's church. These sermons, preached in that ecumenical setting by a Southern Baptist with a distinctive Texas drawl, were an attempt to acknowledge our differences while affirming our common unity in Christ.

Five years later in the pulpit of the Crescent Hill Baptist Church of Louisville, Kentucky, the sermons, rewritten in the light of new developments in the church and the world, were again presented to a congregation composed largely of members of one mammoth American denomination, the Southern Baptist Convention. On this occasion, another summer series, I was concerned that worshipers be able to relate to a larger tradition than that of a peculiarly American, strongly Southern denomination.

In both contexts, however, were persons who listened with patience and responded with affirmation, permitting me to experiment with what for me was a new type of sermon presentation. They were sensitive critics and caring friends who helped me to refine ideas, sharpen style, and participate in some genuine experiences of worship. To the congregations of First Community Church and Crescent Hill Baptist Church I am particularly grateful.

This approach to preaching is not new, and I have been privileged to study with several preacher/historians who modeled this method in lively and creative ways. Professor William R. Estep, Jr., of South-western Baptist Theological Seminary, made church history come to life for me during my early days of theological education. His lecture materials, thorough and precise in their historical analysis, frequently held intriguing elements of the sermonic. Professor Earl Kent Brown of Boston University is a master of the historical sermon. His skill in the pulpit and the classroom unites the historian's craft with that of the accomplished preacher. His style of presentation as well as his ability to blend elements of Scripture, history, and personal faith has had a profound influence upon me. To those two teachers I am greatly indebted.

Much of the historical material for these sermons was presented to unsuspecting students in church history classes at The Southern Baptist Theological Seminary. Their response—positive and negative—was extremely valuable to me. To those students I offer my sincere thanks.

Mrs. Sally Claybrooks coordinated efforts at preparation of the manuscript in the face of my constant revisions. She was patient throughout.

Candyce Leonard, as usual, provided necessary modifications in style and not infrequently challenged the directions of my theology. Stephanie Leonard, our daughter, was an ever-present reminder that the realities of the moment and the promise of the future are as important as the lessons of the past.

1.
Where Are the Clowns?
1 Corinthians 1:18-30

It pleased God through the folly of what we preach to save those who believe.

Judy Collins is right. Sometimes things are so out of joint, so crazy, so foolish that it's all like a big circus. Life, love, and relationships all seem so confusing. And when everything is falling apart, Judy Collins sings hauntingly: "But where are the clowns? There ought to be clowns."[1] She is right. Sometimes the only ones who can give meaning to the meaningless are the clowns.

The more I read the Scriptures, the more I think that this life we call the gospel is often held together for us by nothing but a bunch of clowns, the most surprising, unexpected, and foolish-looking individuals God or anybody else could find.

A silly old man Noah building an ark—it's never gonna rain . . . not that much.

Moses, a murderer with difficulty in speaking . . . say to Pharaoh, "Let my people go."

David, a kid with five smooth stones—"Go out and face a big giant," as my daughter says redundantly.

What of Simon Peter? Perhaps the biggest clown of all. On today and off tomorrow; confessing in the morning of his faith, "You are the Christ, the Son of the living God"; cursing in the darkness of the night, "I never knew the man."

"Yet," says Jesus, "it is upon persons like you, Peter, that I will build my church, and the gates of hell shall not prevail against it." And he called them: tax collectors, revolutionaries, public sinners, and led them in associating with gluttons and winebibbers (and you know about winebibbers, whoever they were).

What about the folks whom Jesus described as citizens of the kingdom? Weak, idealistic clowns, every one: the pure in heart, the merciful, the peacemakers, the poor in spirit, the lame, the blind, the deaf, the poor—clowns all. Surely they are not the stuff of which a church is made. No, give us the strapping athletes and beauty queens, the successful celebrities and the beautiful people in tie-dyed jeans for Jesus! Give us the secure and those who are convinced of their vocational task as builders of the church triumphant. But let the clowns shape up or ship out.

And then there comes the memory of Saint Francis, the madman, the clown, giving up his material goods in poverty, preaching to the poor in simplicity, living with the leper in humility.

Or we recall the scandalous behavior of George Fox. In and out of prison, beaten and berated for his audacious preaching of the light of God in every man and woman.

Or try to tell Martin Luther what a foolish clown he is for challenging the power structure of the church—attacking the very Vicar of Christ himself. Calm down, Luther, you'll never win, you're too introspective, too easily depressed. You've got to think more positively and examine the great possibilities before you. And we hear again his foolishly beautiful words, "My conscience is captive to the Word of God. . . . God help me. Here I stand. Amen."

And what of Lottie Moon who traveled to China to labor for years before anyone believed the gospel?

What a bunch of clowns the old church has been touched, indeed forged, by. They were not always sure of themselves or what they were doing, in fact they were not always sure of the gospel they proclaimed and yet they went on with it.

That brings us to the strange story which Jesus tells about two young men and the father who comes to the first and says, "Go and work today in the vineyard." And immediately the boy replies: "I'll go. I'll go where you want me to go." He said he would, but he didn't. "Lord, I'll go," but he wouldn't. The father goes to the second son and says, "Go and work in my vineyard." The son answers: "I will not go. Not me. I'll do what I want." But somewhere along the way he thought better of it, changed his mind, and went out. "Who was obedient?" Jesus asked his listeners. "The second son," they replied. Then there comes the Word of God. "Tax collectors and prostitutes will enter the kingdom ahead of you. They said no and went their own way but repented and believed. You said yes, but never believed."[2] The unexpected ones, the unlikely ones, the clowns believed and went.

The church is full of many people like those two sons. Multitudes of people who shout from pulpits and baptistries, from summer camps and revival services, "Lord, I'll go. . . ." But for some, the glib answers wear thin, the superficial joy turns sour, and the hurt of it, the shame of it catches up with them and they never really go out to confront the world. **They never seem to doubt, but they never really believe.**

Yet the church also has its share of those who at first cry out, "I'll never go. It's too foolish, too impossible." But somehow they think better of it and take a chance, discovering the pain and the adventure of the gospel. They are the clowns.

That is what this series of sermons is all about. It provides an all too brief examination of some of the most famous "clowns" of Christian history. They lived in different eras, were raised in different circumstances, and confronted different problems. But they heard the Word of God in ways which challenged them, the church, and the world to think new thoughts and attempt new actions. In many respects they seem far removed from us. Their methods appear archaic, their zeal a bit unbalanced, and their theology weak in crucial places. Yet they belong to each of us as those who went before us. In a sense their battles are ours, and their struggles our own. The Word of God which arrested them continues to come to us. The church still needs its share of clowns.

For while our faith may seem terribly secure, our doctrines inerrantly orthodox, and our actions profoundly relevant, there are surely moments when each of us struggles with the validity of the gospel life. For no matter how secure our faith, there may be times when we want to cry out, "I will never go; it is too impossible, too foolish, this gospel of Jesus Christ. It will not work in the real world. It cannot stop all the hate; it cannot end all the wars; it will never change the basic human condition."

Never forget that it is by the foolishness of the preaching of the cross that God has chosen to communicate his good news. You will need to know that when people you have trusted and believed in disappoint you; when you seek to care for others in Christ's name and have that kindness rejected; when your church tears itself apart in petty disputes and "Christian" cruelty; and when it seems no matter how much you care, pray, and hope some people never believe. At such times, remember it is impossible folly, that gospel to which you have responded. Remember that this Jesus you call Christ seems hopeless and horribly unrealistic.

For when we look at the cross it seems we see the greatest folly in the saddest clown of all; and we almost join with the mocking mob, "He saved others, himself, he cannot save." What a clown! The New Testament shows us that the One we call Lord and Savior was a scandal, treated like a common criminal. To identify with him meant sacrifice and separation from friends and family. In a real sense throughout the church's history the cross remains a scandal, and the cost of discipleship is still quite costly. In history and in the present it has seemed, to many, not worth the trouble.

We will go out into a world where a great many folk judge us as irrelevant individuals jousting with windmills and slaying dinosaurs long since dead, if they ever existed at all. Ralph Wood of Wake Forest University wrote recently in *The Christian Century* of his experiences in Italy and his discovery of the triumph of atheism among young Italian secularists. All other views, especially Christianity, are deemed self-delusion. Wood was confronted by a young leftist who sought dialogue by asking if ethics was the essence of true belief.

Wood writes, "When I replied that a merely ethical existence misses what for me is the core and essence of reality—namely, grace and forgiveness, repentance and mercy, providence and mystery—I discovered a stare of massive incomprehension in her eyes."[3] And so will you with many an American secularist. You will speak of grace to persons who have known little; of forgiveness to those who believe they can never be forgiven; and of mystery to those who laugh at your lack of rational faculties. You will be the clown to them. Worthy only of a patronizing, "You don't really believe all that stuff, now do you?"

And sometimes it appears that they may be right. There are times when what we seek to do in Christ's name seems completely useless, futile, and tragically funny—when we do seem to be clowns.

Lee Going and I have been clowns together. Lee was a student at Southern Baptist Seminary who invited me to preach four days in his rural church. It was one July when temperatures in Kentucky reached over a hundred degrees. A tiny old church with tiny old crowds—fifteen was a multitude. It was so hot that people had to go outside in the sun to cool off! The song leader got up in one service and prophetically proclaimed: "If you think it's hot here, wait till you get to hell." A good illustration, perhaps, but not a major point of my sermon. I preached, sweat poured, and people fanned with funeral-home fans. We went home and nothing much happened so as to call it a crusade or anything. Not one person came forward! It all seemed a little crazy. Why do it? Perhaps because those people wanted a "revival" whether anything happened or not. But perhaps because we believe that something does happen when the Word is proclaimed, even when we do not recognize it. Lee Going is an even bigger clown than I. He stayed out there, offering care, Word, and hope in a small community where they need a clown like he is, whether they realize it or not.

There is, after all, something foolishly exciting about proclaiming hope where there is no hope; about discovering love in a world so full of hate; about calling for peace in a world filled with armaments and war; about demanding self-denial in a society obsessed with materialism and success. For suppose that Paul is right and God really has chosen the weak things to confound the wise. Suppose what seems to be the weakness of God is indeed his greatest strength. Suppose it works and the world really belongs to the clowns after all.

I remember in my childhood in Texas, we went most Januarys to the Southwestern Exposition and Fat Stock Show in Fort Worth. My favorite event was the bull-riding, and with the bulls came the clowns in painted faces and baggy pants, hiding in open-ended barrels. They jumped around, fell down, and looked absolutely incapable of anything but stupid antics—until a rider flew off a cavorting bull and then the clowns became dead serious in their efforts to protect the defenseless, sometimes hurting, rider.

Gradually it began to dawn on me. The clowns were just not there to be funny or entertaining. The cowboys and the audience needed them desperately.

Somehow, in the mystery that is God, the world needs us. Oh, we look silly in the baggy pants of our theology, the painted faces of our practice, and the open-ended barrels of our ethics. But there we are in the center ring where some people need to be protected, where others are hurting, and where those who have fallen need the safety of a second chance. And as foolish as it sounds, that's why the vulnerable God/man on the cross could not save himself, and in doing that, saved others.

But now that cross is empty. The soldiers are gone and the grave has been sealed. The hawkers and the vendors, the curious and the morbid have gone home. The circus is over. But where in the world are the clowns? There really ought to be clowns.

Don't worry, they are still here. For somehow in the mystery that is God, the clowns are good news.

Notes

1. Stephen Sondheim, "Send in the Clowns," Revelation Music Publishing Company/Rilting Music Inc., 1973.

2. See Matthew 21:28-32.

3. Ralph C. Wood, " 'Innocents Abroad' No More," *The Christian Century* (July 5-12, 1978), p. 673.

2.
Paul: He Appeared Also to Me
1 Corinthians 15:3-11

Last of all, as to one untimely born, he appeared also to me.

Damascus Road—merely speak of it and the detailed drama of human transformation comes immediately to mind. It is a scene fraught with pathos and mystery, etched so deeply upon the church's memory that such words as *conversion* and *Damascus Road* have become almost synonymous. The images of the event are familiar to each of us: dusty road, sandaled feet, heat from the blazing Palestinian sun. The intense young Pharisee named Saul, moments away from becoming Paul, moves toward Damascus and the fulfillment of his mission. His way seemed perfectly clear, his future terribly secure. The young Saul was a man to be reckoned with. Brilliant, aggressive, and committed, he lived at fever pitch. Intensely orthodox, he possessed the best credentials of religious leadership: Pharisee of the Pharisees, student of the famous rabbi, Gamaliel, secure in his religion and, I believe, quite satisfied with it.

Saul was a company man, climbing the ladder of ecclesiastical success, perhaps to become the next high priest. After all, he was a determined defender of the faith and as such he set out for Damascus, on a day like any other day.

He had to make the journey, at least on that day. There was heresy in the air, and it had to be confronted. Orthodoxy was at stake, and Saul was the duly recognized protector of Hebrew orthodoxy. The followers of the Jesus Way, the devotees of the criminal god, were wreaking havoc among God's elect. They called this wretched Nazarene, "messiah," and were turning many innocent people from the true and only faith. It was idolatry, blasphemy. And anyone who led Israel toward such heresy had to be silenced—permanently if necessary. Stephen found that out, the hard way.

Saul had been there, holding the cloaks of those who stoned the earliest Christian martyr. Perhaps, some have said, the words of Stephen were still ringing in Saul's ears as he marched toward Damascus:

How stubborn you are, heathen still at heart and deaf to the truth! You always fight against the Holy Spirit. Like fathers, like sons. Was there ever a prophet whom your fathers did not persecute? They killed those who foretold the coming of the Righteous One; and now you have betrayed and murdered him, you who received the Law as God's angels gave it to you, and yet have not kept it (Acts 7:51-53, NEB).

And after Stephen . . . Damascus, with letters from the High Priest attesting to his orthodoxy and acknowledging his authority to deal with the Jesus crowd, Saul went forth. Such power was intoxicating. For Saul was discovering the power of the inquisitor, the power of holding life and death in the balance; the power to determine what is good and what is evil in the lives of other human beings. Power is alluring, even in the religiously sincere. Saul, the power broker, the Grand Inquisitor, moves toward Damascus. For error must be eliminated before it pollutes a multitude. Better to stone one blasphemer than have a hundred innocent ones corrupted by the teachings of Jesus. And Saul, Pharisee, devoted Jew, brilliant human being, would decide with amazing clarity what was truth and what was blasphemy.

As he goes, "breathing out threats," he later recalls, Saul is confronted by the presence of that heretical Christ whom he is trying to destroy. "He appeared also to me," Paul wrote, and in those moments, he discovered what we all should know. The intensity of religious convictions does not necessarily make religion true. It is possible to believe a great deal and still not really believe.

As Martin Dibelius writes: Paul realized on the Damascus road that "with the best will in the world to serve God, one can pass him by."[1] Paul would later acknowledge that he had been so zealous for the law and its purity that he almost came to ruin. He confessed to the Thessalonians (2:15) that the logically minded, doctrinaire representatives of the religion of the law killed in their zeal both the Lord Jesus and the prophets.

It can happen to all of us. Conviction turns to legalism, sincerity becomes self-righteousness, and faith moves to dogmatism. Our lives become so overwhelmed by the intensity of *our* doctrines, *our* faith, *our* word, that we cannot detect the movement of God or feel the warm winds of the Holy Spirit blowing afresh and anew. Sometimes we become so obsessed that we can tolerate no deviation from our own self-determined religious norms. Thus we may never hear the Word of God, even on Damascus. Many speak the Word of God, use it, and proclaim it, yet never hear it for themselves.

Suppose Saul had not obeyed the Christ who appeared to him. Suppose he had walked away. Oh, we say, it was irresistible, that grace of God which overpowered him. He could not but say yes to the light shining in his eyes and the warmth throbbing in his heart. But others had. Remember that young man full of the Law, obedient from his youth, who met the living Christ, flesh and blood? He was touched by the demands of the gospel but stayed with the Law and his possessions. Jesus appeared to that wealthy ruler, who considered the cost and walked away.

Perhaps Saul might have done that. He might have turned from this new mission back to the shrill, power-mad blast of heresy hunting and the security of tedious tradition.

"Saul, you have Abraham for a father—defend that true faith, stone and silence the heretics, think of your future. You only go round once in life and you must grab for all the kingdom, the power, and the glory you can get. Do not be deterred by voices and visions, impossible dreams and distant drummers. Stay safe, sincere, and powerful. Cling to the religion of answers, formulas, and procedures."

But Saul gave it all up—all the power, all the possibilities, all the potential for which he had been born and bred. Years later he loved to remember those times, those credentials, and recount them to Christian believers, naming his abilities and reflecting on his zeal.

Perhaps that was a particular weakness of his personality or perhaps he came to appreciate that which Israel and the law meant at one early stage in his life, grateful that it was a beginning, not an end, "a schoolmaster to lead us to Christ," he called it. But even when he remembered his training, his credentials, and his zeal for the law, he would also add, "I count it all loss for the excellency of the knowledge of Christ Jesus my Lord."

So the question comes: Has he appeared also to you? And if he has, what does that mean about the response of your own life to God? Like Paul, we have only one life. At some point, each of us must decide which of the visions of life we will choose. We are likewise confronted by the responsibility which we bear for our own zeal and our private battles for the faith. We are, all of us, ever living with the uneasy reality that in God's sight our orthodoxy may be heresy, and our heresy may turn out to be truth.

Thus we recognize something else about those moments on Damascus Road—that God is ever choosing unexpected places and surprising people to communicate his good news. In our text, Paul recounts the anticipated and unanticipated appearances of the resurrected Christ—to Peter and the twelve, to five hundred believers, to James and to the other apostles. The crucified Christ became the risen Lord and made himself known to fishermen and tax collectors, public sinners and other unexpected persons outside the law, whom Saul felt to be beyond the complete grace of God. He appeared first to friends and followers, and, Paul writes, while he was at it, this risen Christ appeared also to me.

And that is the mystery of it—that he appears to the likes of Saul and us. He is the Christ who ever takes us by surprise. The God who appeared to Saul is the kind of God who goes after people while they are in the process of doing him dirty. And suddenly Saul realized that being a Pharisee of the Pharisees does not help one little bit to make you right with God. As Frederick Buechner says, "God did business with you not because of who you were but because of who *he* was." When he least expected it, Saul is brought to the realization that "no matter who you are or what you have done, God wants you on his side."[2] You do not have to do anything or be anything. It is God who justifies, and realizing that is the first step toward being saved.

And Paul who used to be Saul utilized a dramatic phrase to describe the surprise of it all. "I am," he insists, "as one born out of due time. This birth of mine was monstrous, untimely born." It was like a breech birth—one unexpected and difficult, one you would never have dreamed possible except by the unfathomable grace of God.

Isn't that the same with all of us? Aren't we all untimely born? Not one of us is worthy of the gospel. We are all a surprise. And until we accept our own untimely births we may not understand just how radical is that word we call good news. "He appeared also to me, even me, " Paul said, in the unexpected people and places of the world.

Of all the people in the world, no one would have guessed that the Grand Inquisitor would wind up surrendering for the mission field—that Saul the Powerful would identify himself irrevocably with Jesus, the suffering servant.

The gospel is ever coming to us as a big surprise. Paul thought he knew who the enemy was—the sect of the Nazarene—be done with them and the faith will be saved. The church thought it knew who its enemy was—Saul the persecutor—"doomed and damned to a devil's hell," as the New Testament revivalists must have said. And God set all of them on their ears. Saul gets converted, and the church gets a new apostle, and neither of them bought it at first. Look at Saul, instead of having his eyes opened by Jesus like so many before him, he goes blind. It is too much for him. Finally his eyes are opened as all things begin to become new. What a surprise!

And what about the church? They were scared to death of him—thought it was a plot to infiltrate their ranks. And you cannot really blame them. Paul's conversion would be like a Ku Klux Klan Grand Dragon on his way to a cross burning with hood over his face and a gasoline can in his hand showing up at an NAACP meeting and saying, "Brother, how much are the membership dues? I am one of you." And the brothers respond: "Beat it, turkey."

But sure enough, it happened and God strained the early church beyond its wildest imagination. If Saul gets in . . . anybody can. "He appeared also to me," Paul said, and the church has not been the same since.

And again we feel the foolishness of the gospel. It does not always work like any of us think it should and it sometimes seems to go where we never thought it could and do what we never dreamed possible. Sometimes the heresy hunters get converted and sometimes the heretics turn out to be the real believers after all. And God surprises all of us by appearing to people you and I want to ignore, avoid, and keep outside our nice churches.

The people who are most miserable are often the ones who go through life ruling out those kinds of unbelievable and inconsistent surprises as impossible for the living God. We are so often blind to the gift of the gospel in others or so blinded by our own experience with

Christ that we cannot see that other eyes have been opened and other lives made whole. Sometimes the gospel must come to us as bad news, shocking news, before it is good. We realize that what we thought would save us, won't, and what we thought could never save us, does. You and I need to be ready and willing to be surprised by the amazing grace of God when it shows up in the impossible people and events of our living.

And therein may rest Paul's greatest gift. It is not that Jesus appeared only to him. Because of his battles, you and I know the good news that Christ has come also to us, and we do not have to become Jews in the process. Damascus Road belongs to all of us. Oh, we probably won't hear voices or see visions. But the confession of Saul become Paul is a confession to which we are all called. He appeared also to me and you and you.

He appears to us and suddenly we, like Saul, discover more questions, problems, and pain than we ever dreamed possible. But we also discover newness as never before. I, yet not I. I am the same, but I am not. And the life I now live, I live by faith in the Son of God. All of my life is affected. I am always being shocked, surprised, and astounded with what God does and asks me to do. For he appears to me in the most impossible events and circumstances.

He appeared to that crowd that first believed: to Peter and the twelve, to five hundred, and to the other apostles. He appeared also to the worst of all possible candidates: zealous, brilliant, bigoted, sinner, Saul of Tarsus. And if he did that, surely he can also appear to each one of us. Honest he can. Well, can't he?

Notes

1. Martin Dibelius, *Paul* (Philadelphia: Westminster Press, 1953), p. 63.
2. Frederick Buechner, *Wishful Thinking* (New York: Harper & Row, Publishers, 1973), p. 49.

Selected Bibliography

BARCLAY, WILLIAM. *Ambassador for Christ: The Life and Teaching of Paul.* Valley Forge, PA.: Judson Press, 1974.

BORNKAMM. GUNTHER. *Paul.* New York: Harper and Row, 1971.

DIBELIUS, MARTIN. *Paul.* Philadelphia: Westminster, 1953.

GRANT, MICHAEL. *Saint Paul.* London: Weidenfeld and Nicolson, 1976.

RAINES, ROBERT. *To Kiss the Joy.* Waco: Word Books, 1973.

SANDMEL, SAMUEL. *The Genius of Paul.* New York: Farrar, Straus and Cudahy, 1958.

STENDAHL, KRISTER. *Paul Among Jews and Gentiles.* Philadelphia: Fortress Press, 1976.

3.
Francis of Assisi:
Peace and Poverty
Matthew 10:5-20,39

He who finds his life will lose it, and he who loses his life for my sake will find it.

In some respects he seems very modern and familiar to us, this one called Francis. Pampered son of the middle class, he brashly sowed his wild oats, radically repudiating the values of his parents. Alienated from his father, he sought youthful fame and fortune only to find disillusionment with the ways of the world. Yet in other ways he is of another day and time, a medieval man, foreign to all we know and much we treasure. He rejected education and material goods as destructive to the gospel life and was fanatically and irrationally committed to poverty. Eating garbage from the streets, begging in the name of Christ, he had no home, no assets, no life insurance policy, no clothes but the rags on his back. He received visions from God, experienced in some mystical ecstasy the stigmata as marks appeared on his hands and feet reminiscent of the wounds of the crucified Christ. Worst of all, some will say, he was a Roman Catholic bound by what appears to many as limitless dogma and tedious tradition. He seems eccentric at best, certifiably mad at worst. His life is legend, myth, romantic epic, so sentimentalized that it seems impossible to know anything true about him. Yet he speaks to us about the presence of the Spirit in a human life, the life of the gospel itself, and the power of the word of God. Perhaps we can hear that word again, for ourselves, through Francis of Assisi.

He was christened Giovanni in the old church in Assisi, Italy, in 1182 but his father, Pietro, a prominent cloth merchant, nicknamed him Francis, in admiration for France, the land of the troubadour poets. As a youth Francis was pampered by his parents, and sought pleasure at every turn. Some call him a "master of revels," a playboy who spent much time in drinking, joking and prankish activities, squandering great sums of money, emulating the behavior of the French troubadours who roamed the countryside singing of romance and chivalry. He had his first opportunity to achieve his own dreams of glory when at age twenty he went off to war against a neighboring city-state. The Assisian army was severely defeated; Francis was captured and imprisoned for a year.

Upon returning home he fell gravely ill, hovering near death for weeks. This suffering began an emotional transformation in Francis. His conversion was not sudden, in some cataclysmic rapture, but occurred through a series of developing events and impressions on his life.

The young man seemed overcome by restlessness, dissatisfied with his former revels, indifferent to work in his father's cloth shop, disillusioned about the glories of war. He made a pilgrimage to Rome in hopes of finding some remedy for his despondency. There he was accosted by multitudes of beggars who jammed the Roman streets. Repulsed and yet attracted by them he exchanged his fine clothes for a beggar's rags and walked the streets pleading for alms—humiliating behavior for a merchant's son.

Returning to Assisi, Francis experienced another incident leading to his conversion. Riding one day, he met a leper, one of the most feared and shunned men of the time. To look at such physical decay sickened him, but somehow he was compelled to care for the man. Dismounting, he gave the leper alms and kissed his hand, receiving back the kiss of peace, defeating his own repulsion at human suffering. It was the beginning of his long ministry to these outcasts of society. It was the beginning of his service to God.

Soon there came a second dramatic experience. While praying in the old dilapidated chapel of Saint Damian, it is said that he heard a voice from the cross saying: "My house is being destroyed; go therefore and repair it for me." At last he had a cause! He would rebuild this crumbling edifice!

Of course, we say, there is a deeper meaning to this vision. All of God's church needed rebuilding with the new life of the Spirit. But Francis was not mature enough to see this wider perspective. He was just beginning to discover God's presence in his life. Rebuilding one church was cause enough.

He needed money and where better to get it than in his papa's shop?

He rushed home, sold his horse and several bales of cloth from the family business, making the sign of the cross over the confiscated articles to indicate their sacred purpose. Needless to say, Papa Bernardone was less than pleased. His worthless son had gone completely mad. Father seized son, dragged him home, beat him, and locked him in a closet for several days. When this failed to produce the necessary repentance, and since the youth was babbling about God and heavenly voices, Francis's father took him to the Bishop of Assisi. The bishop was kind but firm, full of that sanctimonious advice which the church too often uses to pour cold water on the fiery attitudes of its prophets. "Now hold on, my son," he said. "Your mission is good, but your method inappropriate. God does not want you to go against your father."

But Francis was ready with an answer for father and bishop. In a flare for the dramatic which characterized his entire life he announced: "Until this time I have called Pietro Bernardone my father, now I am the servant of God. Not only the money but everything that can be called his I will return to my father, even the very clothes which he has given me." And with the speed of a medieval streaker, the fervent young man cast off all his clothes, commenting, "Now I will say only our Father which art in heaven."[1]

It was, you must admit, a decisive act. Away he went in borrowed clothes, singing the praises of God in the tunes of the French minstrels. He cared for lepers and worked for three years rebuilding the old church outside Assisi, wearing the clothes of a beggar, eating garbage from the gutters, singing, always singing, praise to God.

And gradually it began to dawn on him. He began to realize that he was called of God to rebuild something more than one old church. Something, G. K. Chesterton says, that has often enough fallen into ruin but has never been past rebuilding. A church that could always be built anew though it had rotted away to its first foundation stone against which the gates of hell cannot prevail—the Church of Jesus Christ.[2]

He rebuilt other churches around Assisi and in one of them, in February 1209, the broader vision of his mission was made clear to him. While at worship, he listened to the reading from Matthew's Gospel, "Go and preach the kingdom of Heaven. Heal the sick, cleanse the leper, cast out demons. . . . Go without gold, silver, purse, shoes, coat or staff. . . . Be sheep in the midst of wolves, . . . but fear not, for the

Spirit of your father speaks through you."

It was as if God had spoken to Francis and to him alone. "No one showed me what I should do," he said, "but the most high God himself revealed to me how I must live according to the teachings of the Holy Gospel."[3] And he sought to do just that . . . literally. He discarded sandals for bare feet, and wore only a rough garment tied with a piece of rope. "The Lord give you peace" was his greeting as he went about preaching, not in eloquence, but in simplicity and honesty. He did not sermonize but called his listeners to love and fear God and repent of their sins. Some laughed and ridiculed him, others listened, and some began to follow.

One biographer writes: "Braving all ridicule, he stood in the squares of Assisi and nearby towns and preached the gospel of poverty and Christ. . . . Revolted by the unscrupulous pursuit of wealth that marked the age, and shocked by the splendor and luxury of some clergymen, he denounced money itself as a devil and a curse and bade his followers despise it."[4]

Soon a small group of the "Little Brothers," as Francis called them, had gathered about him. They wore coarse brown robes, lived in arbors made of branches, went out barefoot, without money, and preached the gospel of repentance. They cared for lepers, slept in the streets, and when they returned tired and discouraged, Francis washed their feet, fed them, and preached to them the joys of the kingdom. He called them beyond materialism and dogma to the message of Christ: repent, believe the gospel, and do good. The Franciscans had begun, and the church would never be the same.

Now all that is well and good for the Middle Ages, or the Catholics, or dusty old church historians, but what do Francis and the Word of God which came to him have to do with Protestants, secularists, or worldly evangelicals who inhabit the latter days of the twentieth century?

First, Francis says something to us about the gospel and poverty. If there was any hate in his heart, it was for materialism and if there was a love affair, it was with Lady Poverty. He saw how concern for things material had separated him from his own father, how obsession with money could turn one's vision from the needs of others to the fulfillment of self-interest. He looked at the church of his day with its vast wealth and endowments, its manor houses and serfs and called that church to return to the Savior who had no place to lay his head.

He became *il poverello,* the little poor man, warning his followers not to accept pay for their work, believing that the fewer one's possessions the freer one was to serve God. "If we possess property," he said, "we should need arms to defend it. Property is the source of quarrels and lawsuits, and is an obstacle to love of God and one's neighbor."[5]

Francis's obsession with poverty was an overstatement which few can share with him. We do not exalt him as the example of the way all are to live. But in his overstatement, his hatred for things material, and his proclamation of the good news to the poor, he calls us to take seriously the gospel of Jesus Christ.

Along with celebration, frivolity, and foolishness, Francis was everlastingly serious. He teaches us that the gospel can and must be taken seriously. Jesus was not merely an idealistic dreamer, a new legalist, or a mechanical, inhuman god-in-a-box. His teaching did not merely apply to twelve first-century apostles. It was and is a way of life which can and must be lived. For Francis and for each of us sacrifice is no game, no affectation, no protest. It is the calling of those who follow the Christ who emptied himself and became of no reputation.

Thus we discover that the gospel is indeed the scandal of identifying with the lepers, the rejects, and the unclean among us. Like Francis, we must seek out the lepers of our world, the persons our world shuns, and embrace them with the love of Christ. Who are the lepers in your world? The thief whose skin is black, or the Klansman whose skin is white? Their wounds need cleansing. Their hurts need healing. Can we take seriously our calling to the lepers all around us?

Francis's rags were not the rags of false piety but the common dress of the poor. His poverty was not a badge of his own holiness but his identification with the outcasts of the world. It was as if he chose to live in the rat-infested ghettos of modern slums, bringing hope and humanity to the dehumanized existence of the urban poor. Poverty was not romance but the stark reality of hunger, cold, and suffering.[6] Francis's deeds were also more than humanitarian paternalism, more than pity for the underprivileged. It was his way of saying to the poor, "The gospel of Christ belongs here, with you. The love of Christ is needed here." Jesus Christ himself has become poor. Christ is starving; Christ wears rags; Christ embraces lepers; indeed, he is the leper!

Francis shows us that Jesus' teachings can have an impact on our lives. It is easy to say they are inspired, inerrant, or absolutely true but it is agony to hear them for ourselves and allow them to change the way we live. Listen to some of those hard sayings. "If you would be perfect, go sell all you have, give to the poor, and come, and follow me." "If any man would come after me let him deny himself, take up his cross daily, and follow me." "Freely you have received, freely give."

Jesus' word to us is that discipleship is costly and demanding. It calls us to reject obsession with materialism, the goddess of success, and the "master charge mentality" which suggests that happiness is found not in human relationships but in carrying economic and social clout. The gospel calls us away from all which blinds us to persons or chains us to goals which undermine our calling as the serving people of God. Francis reminds us that the gospel of Christ is not a doctrine which we codify and protect, not an observance we perform, not an excuse for excessive wealth. It is a life we live by faith in the God who identifies himself with the poor and the oppressed.

Second, Francis reminds us that all God's creatures are to live together in peace. When the Catholic Church was organizing a crusade against the infidel muslims—to kill one was a service to God and to die on a Christian crusade brought assurance of heaven—Francis was an instrument of God's peace. With great hardship he walked to the Eastern empire of the muslims and preached to them the gospel of peace. Even the great leader Saladin received him as a man of peace and love.

Again he seems the irrelevant idealist, for no one was saved and the holy wars continued. In the midst of all that hatred, Francis brought a prophetic word of love. In a world gone mad fighting wars in the name of God, Francis's was a word of peace. Such peacemakers are needed in our world and those called to the gospel are called to be peacemakers.

Peace for us must not be an idle dream. That we as God's people are peacemakers and that peace is the will of God for his creation are basic to the biblical witness. In a world where so many have put great faith in nuclear armaments can we not as Christ's church call for a greater faith in God? In our world the peacemakers are no longer the naive and idealistic ones. There is no victory, only devastation and indescribable suffering, if we continue to prepare for nuclear warfare. Can we take seriously the biblical teaching about peacemakers and the kingdom of God? The gospel word of peace and poverty which Francis discovered for his day, we must discover for our own time.

Oh, we say, it is a nice story, but it is not relevant for us. We cannot sell all we have. We cannot beg or preach to our enemies. We cannot escape taxes, mortgages, and family commitments. And after all he is a Catholic and they seem obsessed with dogma and ritual, traditions and creeds. They cannot really speak to us, "the people of the Book." Yet in the spring of 1979, the Pope of that Church returned to his native Poland and in the face of totalitarian oppression proclaimed the freedom of the human spirit liberated by faith in Christ. The people braved government sanctions to hear him preach, to sing songs of praise to God, and affirm for all the world to see the spirit of faith in the midst of a Marxist materialistic state. Sometimes by God's grace the people of dogma can become the people of the Spirit.

While that was going on, Southern Baptists and other Protestant groups were being torn apart by debates over dogma and our voice of personal, transforming experience with Jesus Christ was dimmed and dulled. Sometimes the people of the Spirit can become a people trapped by dogma.

Relevant? Francis may be especially relevant to modern Christians, for he belongs to all of us. He calls us again to the freedom of the living Christ and the awesome, exciting authority of the Word of God which can transform us from shallow dogmatists into committed disciples. For at the foundation of our faith it is not merely that we have a firm hold on all the truths of the Bible but that the truths of the Bible have a firm hold on us. It is less that the Bible be taken dogmatically than that it be taken seriously in the way we live.

Let us at worship hear and obey Jesus' words of challenge and adventure: "If any one will come after me, let him deny himself, take up his cross daily, and follow me." From Jesus to Francis to each one of us, that is the Word of God. Who among us will dare to take it seriously?

Notes

1. Paul Sabatier, *Life of St. Francis* (New York: Charles Scribner's Sons, 1894), p. 61.

2. G. K. Chesterton, *St. Francis of Assisi* (Garden City: Image Books, 1957), p. 58.

3. "The Testament of St. Francis" in Leo Sherley-Price, *St. Francis of Assisi* (New York: Harper and Brothers, 1959), p. 201.

4. Will Durant, *The Age of Faith* (New York: Simon and Schuster, 1950), p. 795.

5. Sabatier, pp. 80-81.

6. Lawrence Cunningham, *Brother Francis, An Anthology of Writings By and About St. Francis* (New York: Harper and Row Publishers, 1972), p. xiii.

Selected Bibliography

CHESTERTON, G. K. *St. Francis of Assisi.* Garden City: Image Books, 1957.

CUNNINGHAM, LAWRENCE. *Brother Francis, and Anthology of Writing By and About St. Francis.* New York: Harper and Row Publishers, 1972.

FRANCESCO D'ASSISI. *The Little Flowers and the Life of St. Francis with the Mirror of Perfection.* New York: E. P. Dutton and Co., 1912.

SABATIER, PAUL. *Life of St. Francis.* New York: Charles Scribner's Sons, 1894.

SMITH, JOHN HOLLAND. *Francis of Assisi.* New York: Charles Scribner's Sons, 1972.

4.

Martin Luther: Captive to the Word
Romans 10:11-17

Every one who calls upon the name of the Lord will be saved.

In 1521, Martin Luther stood before the Holy Roman Emperor and other leaders of church and state to answer charges of heresy regarding his views. Johann von Eck, the brilliant Catholic theologian, confronted him: "Martin, how can you assume that you are the only one to understand scripture? Would you put your judgment above that of so many famous men and claim that you know more than they all?" "I ask you, Martin, answer candidly . . . do you repudiate your books and the errors they contain?" And suddenly the words were pouring from Luther's lips: "Unless I am convinced by Scripture and plain reason—I do not accept the authority of popes and councils, for they have contradicted each other—my conscience is captive to the Word of God. I cannot and I will not recant anything, for to go against conscience is neither safe nor right. God help me, here I stand. Amen."[1]

Captive to the Word of God. . . . What is it that would make an individual stand alone on conscience and the Word of God when all the world and its traditions said that he was wrong? For Martin Luther, it was not the first time he had felt alone, with only the wrath and mercy of God before him. Years before, as a young law student, Luther had another lonely and terrifying encounter. While he was returning to the university after a visit with parents, a severe thunderstorm descended upon Luther's path. But the youth was oblivious to the rain, the thunder, and the lightning, for he was wrestling with another storm raging within himself. He had intended to inform his father that he could not continue his law studies, that his interests lay elsewhere. But his father had been so proud, so filled with plans for his aspiring young son, that Martin had been unable to tell him. Suddenly his thoughts were interrupted as a bolt of lightning cracked from the sky, knocking him to the ground. In terror he cried out, "Saint Anna, help me, I will become a monk." The man was spared but the vow had been made. He returned to the university, gave one last party for his friends, and some two weeks later, entered the monastery of the Augustinian Hermits at Erfurt.[2]

He had not made his decision in a vacuum. Numerous influences from his family, his church, and within himself had brought Luther to the monastery. Born in 1483, Martin was the son of Hans Luther, a miner who had risen from peasant stock and desired that his son achieve an even higher social status as a lawyer. Thus he had worked hard to pay for Martin's university education. Luther had much respect for his domineering father, and their estrangement over his decision to enter the monastery hurt Martin deeply. Of his mother we know relatively little except that she was somewhat typical of the superstitious Germans of the sixteenth century who saw the woods as filled with elves and spirits and who blamed the devil for cracked eggs and soured milk. She taught him one of his first rhymes: "If folk don't like you and me, the fault with us is like to be."[3]

Luther himself was an intelligent child devoted to his studies, fond of music, and proficient on the lute. He loved the beauty of the German countryside with its great trees and hills, but was subject to excessive periods of doubt and depression. These moments haunted him throughout his life—times when he felt that he could hardly live with his depression and fears. This state of mind was often aided by the religion of his day. For Luther's concern was not for the things of this world, but of the next, and church often contributed to his fear of damnation and the wrath of God.

Roland Bainton says that the concerns of the sixteenth-century church and its influence on Luther can be illustrated in the stained-glass windows, woodcuts, and images typical of those in German cathedrals. For in a society where few could read and where few books existed, religion and the Scriptures were often taught through the use of pictures and drawings. One such woodcut depicted Christ as the judge—fair and just, cold and severe. Christ was in the center of the drawing, seated on a rainbow, consigning the righteous to heaven and the unrighteous to hell. A close look at the heaven-bound throng revealed a number of

monks, priests, and nuns who by their holy works had received
salvation. Each could say, "This is what I have done for salvation."
Luther realized that for himself he had nothing to show in order to gain
salvation from a just and fearful God. Thus, like so many of his day,
Luther was convinced that only as a clergyman was salvation insured,
and he entered the monastery driven primarily by a desire to save his
own soul.[4]

Bainton suggests that Luther tried three approaches to satisfy his
religious struggles with the monastery. The first was in observance of the
basic monastic way of life. Initially, this brought much contentment, for
his religious nature thrived on the life of meditation and devotion. There
was prayer seven times a day, contemplation, manual labor, and study.
All looked well until he was confronted with another thunderstorm of
the spirit: his first mass.

It should have been a time of great significance, for in this act,
Catholics believed, Luther did what was unique above all others. By the
words of institution he performed the miracle which transformed bread
and wine into the very body and blood of Jesus Christ. Luther's father,
still displeased with him, was present. As the service began all went well
until he reached the words, "We offer unto thee the only true God."
Suddenly Martin was struck by God's majesty and wrath. How could
he, sinful man, address a holy God? With trembling hand and terrified
heart, he completed the service only to face his father who delivered the
final blow. The father denounced Martin and the monastery for his son's
failure to honor his father and mother. Luther asserted in self-defense:
"But, Father, I was called of God in the thunderstorm!" To which his
father replied in words which haunt many a minister: "God grant that
your call was not an apparition of the devil!" In this experience the
security of the monastery was destroyed and the inner struggle
intensified.[5]

Next, Luther turned for salvation to the path of self-help. If seven
prayers a day were good, fourteen should be better; if one day's fast
helped, three should really avail. Often his fellow monks found Luther
on the cold floor of his cell, naked and unconscious after hours of self-
denial and prayer. At confession he listed every minute sin. Finally, his
confessor remarked half jokingly: "Stop all these petty confessions.
Next time see that you have some good juicy sin to confess, like

adultery or murder."[6] But with Luther it was no joke. Always he asked: "Have I fasted enough?" "Am I humble enough?" And still there was no peace. Indeed, he confessed that he hated this just and righteous God.

Thus he turned to a third way for salvation within the church. It was sought in the lives of the saints whose good deeds benefited the salvation of those whose lives lacked the necessary merit. Thus, by making pilgrimages, viewing relics of the saints, even paying money, a sinner could move toward salvation through the merits of more holy men and women.

He went to Rome, where there was more opportunity to earn the merit of the saints than anywhere else in the world. Luther tried to take advantage of every opportunity: visiting shrines, saying mass, and even wishing his own parents were dead since it was easier to pray them out of purgatory in Rome than back in Germany. He deplored the immorality of the Roman clergy and their irreverence for holy things. He returned to Germany, disillusioned with his church and its way of salvation.

The doubts and depression continued. All his efforts at securing salvation had failed. Staupitz, his superior in the monastery, loved Luther dearly and sought to help. Staupitz advised: "Fasten your eyes on Christ who has made provision for your real sins." He encouraged Luther to take his doctor's degree and begin teaching at the university, preach every Sunday, and direct the affairs of the order. "Luther," he said, "cure yourself by curing others."[7]

So Martin began to teach at the new university at Wittenberg and his teaching led him to the Bible and the Bible led him to a new life. He lectured on Psalms and discovered a God both just and loving. He taught Romans and found that "there is no condemnation to those that are in Christ Jesus." From Hebrews he read that we have no priest save Christ himself; and from Galatians he learned of the freedom whereby Christ has set us free. Gradually he realized that Jesus, too, had known loneliness and depression. Had he not cried out from the cross, "My God, why has thou forsaken me?" Christ had been forsaken. He was not removed from us. He was with us. As Bainton writes, "The judge upon the rainbow had become the derelict upon the cross."[8] And ultimately, on some unknown day, while reading the words of Romans 1:17, "The just shall live by faith," he came to discover that a merciful

God justifies men and women by faith; that our faith in Christ accomplishes reconciliation with God so that God no longer counts our sin against us.[9]

He wrote: "There I began to understand that the righteousness of God is that by which the righteous lives by a gift of God, namely by faith. . . . Here I felt that I was altogether born again, and had entered paradise itself through open gates."[10] The righteousness of God he formerly hated and feared, now he came to love. Luther was overtaken by the very living Word of God, discovering that through trusting faith, merciful God receives sinful men and women.

It was that discovery which led him in October 1517, to challenge the very foundation of the church of his day, a church which sincerely believed that it was the only rightful interpreter of the Word of God. It alone had truth and tolerated no deviancy from it. To dispute prevailing dogmas was to be branded a heretic and face the consequences. Better to burn one heretic than to have him or her corrupt a multitude from the truth. The fires burned, the heretics were offered up while the church preached its dogma and talked the language of the Scripture.

The church possessed orthodoxy but its values had become so bound to the culture of the age that few could separate the church from the world. This audacious German monk cried out to the pious protectors of orthodoxy: "You read the Scripture but you know little of the Word of God." "You believe many doctrines but your worship is worldly and shallow." The Word of God through Martin Luther confronted the church of his day.

It was rough going, for the popular religion of the time was comfortably established, lucrative, and exceptionally pious. The selling of indulgences, the purchase of "eternal security," was not merely to raise money or delude people. Many of the preachers and most of the faithful sincerely believed it was a godly act. The indulgence sellers no doubt felt they were preaching the Word of God. They gave moving sermons on purgatory, punishment, and possibility; threw in a few death bed stories; and concluded with a poem of hope: "When a coin in the coffer clings, a soul from purgatory springs." People were moved, response was overwhelming, and surely God was glorified.

The indulgence sellers believed what many of us mistakenly believe. The common folk cannot handle the Word of God for themselves. They need some formula, some package deal, which aids their simple faith and prevents any doubt. The indulgences were merely tools which led persons to salvation. After all, the ends do justify the means, as long as it is for God.

And to this popular religion came the Word of God through Luther on that All Hallow's eve. God does not trick or treat people into heaven. "The just shall live by faith." Salvation is the gift of God, not of works. And God can be trusted to touch even the ignorant peasant with his Word.

There is a lot of pop religion around today claiming to have a corner on the Word of God. But instead of a theology of the Word it is more like a Gypsy-Rose-Lee theology, a you-gotta-have-a-gimmick faith in a let-me-entertain-you religion, based on media hype, celebrities, and Hollywood hucksters. A lot of it centers around the old cliche, "It doesn't matter how you get a man or a woman to Jesus as long as you get them there." Well, it does matter how you get a man or a woman to Jesus. If the gospel has something to do with ethics and discipleship, it matters. And the means we use to present the Word of God will say a great deal about the Word of God we present. For it is possible to preach a very nice religion without preaching the Word of God.

Beware when you call the church from its gimmicks back to the Word. You, like Luther, may be declared a heretic and a disturber of the theological peace. The Word of God is ever disturbing and judging God's church. For Luther reminds us that the church must be captive to the Word.

The Word of God, Paul says, is God speaking to men and women. By the Word, faith is awakened in our lives. The Word moves through the medium of Scripture and the mouth of the messenger to become a living presence in the eternal *now* of the gospel. To believe we must hear; to hear we must be informed. But not all who hear believe. Paul writes that "faith is awakened by the message and the message that awakens it comes through the Word of Christ." We can hear words about God. We can shower people with doctrines and formulas, with four or forty spiritual laws, but ultimately it is God alone who awakens persons to the good news which is the gospel. The Spirit breathes on the ancient Word and speaks anew in every age.

Luther wrote: "For the preaching of the gospel is nothing else than Christ coming to us or we being brought to him." "I have let the word of God act . . . it is all powerful, it takes hearts prisoner, and when they are taken prisoner the work which is done comes from the word itself."[11] And, he insisted, if only one person is changed by the Word of the gospel, it is worthy of shaking the foundations of the whole world.

This understanding of the Word of God means in one sense that the Word works in and of itself beyond the character or intention of the proclaimer or the listeners. Frank Stagg once reminded me that in the South, churches were singing the words, "red and yellow, black and white, they are precious in his sight," long before they practiced that word. But the power of the Word of God transcended the culture and became a reality through those who demanded that such words about human relationships be lived as well as sung. The Word was and is stronger than our consistency to it. The Word of God does not depend on our character or our theology to be true, real, or powerful. For if it really is God's Word, then every time it is proclaimed something happens to the preacher, the people, and to God.

The elusive Word of God confronts us in our worship. We come for many different reasons, with so many different hurts. Some of us come, as did Luther, with the deepest depressions of life upon us. Some come with ecstatic joy, others bearing sickness and death, others with indifference and cynicism. Worship must be a place where the Word of God speaks to us in every facet of our lives.

When we realize that it is not by might, power, or sophistication but by God's Spirit, perhaps we will stop trying to manipulate the Word or defend it and we will let it go where it will. Perhaps we will even allow the Word of God to transform us. For in captivity to the Word of God we are free—free to minister, care, and live as vehicles of God's Word.

Martin Luther lived a life of turmoil. His struggles with depression did not end until his death. He was an ex-priest who married an ex-nun, and together they had six children. That, if nothing else, is Reformation!

It may be that one day you will stand alone before the officials of church, government, or society and they will say to you: "What gives *you* the right to stand against the popular and orthodox opinions of the day?" Martin Luther's response was as one captive to the Word of God. What holds you captive?

Notes

1. Roland Bainton, *Here I Stand* (New York: Mentor Books, 1950), p. 144. I am grateful to Professor Earl Kent Brown of Boston University for his lectures on Luther.

2. John Dillenberger, ed. *Martin Luther: Selections from His Writings* (Garden City: Anchor Books, 1961), p. xiv.

3. Bainton, *Here I Stand*, p. 18.

4. Ibid., pp. 21-25.

5. Dillenberger, *Martin Luther*, p. xv, and Martin Luther, *Works*, Theodore G. Tappert, ed., vol. 54 (Philadelphia: Fortress Press, 1967), p. 234.

6. Bainton, *Here I Stand*, p. 41. I have rephrased Bainton's translation of this statement.

7. Ibid., pp. 42-45, and Edwin P. Booth, *Martin Luther, Oak of Saxony* (New York: Round Table Press, 1933), p. 66.

8. Ibid., p. 47.

9. Some of the ideas in this section are from Earl Kent Brown, unpublished lecture notes, Boston University.

10. Dillenberger, *Martin Luther*, p. 11.

11. Gerhard Ebeling, *Luther: An Introduction to His Thought* (Philadelphia: Fortress Press, 1972), pp. 66-67, citing W.A. 10.3; 18, 8-19, 7. 11-13 (1522).

Selected Bibliography

BAINTON, ROLAND. *Here I Stand*. New York: Mentor Books, 1950.

BOOTH, EDWIN P. *Martin Luther, Oak of Saxony*. New York: Round Table Press, 1933.

DILLENBERGER, JOHN, ed. *Martin Luther, Selections from His Writings*. Garden City: Anchor Books, 1961.

EBELING, GERHARD. *Luther: An Introduction to His Thought*. Philadelphia: Fortress Press, 1972.

Wood, A. SKEVINGTON. *Captive to the Word*. Grand Rapids: Eerdmans Publishing Co., 1969.

5.
George Fox: The Light Within
John 1:1-14

The light shines in the darkness, and the darkness has not overcome it.

Suppose the choir has just completed a beautiful and inspiring anthem. You admire the candles flickering on the communion table, the flowers, and serenity of worship in a beautiful church building. The minister advances to the pulpit, and you settle back comfortably for a good sermon or a short nap. Suddenly from beneath the balcony one rises to his feet dressed in leather breeches, his strange-looking hat clamped tightly upon his head. Loudly the stranger cries: "Do you dare call this steeple house a church? Do you dare call this multitude of sinners a church? The true church is the pillar and ground of the truth, made up of living stones, living members, a spiritual household, which Christ is the head of; but he is not the head of this mixed multitude or of an old house made up of lime, stones, and wood."[1] He then turns his attention to the pulpit: "Come down you deceiver, you bid people come freely and take the water of life freely and yet you take money for preaching the Scriptures to them. Do you not blush with shame?[2]

The minister blushes with shame and you wake up. Someone calls the police and they cart the stranger off to jail for disturbing the peace while the congregation resumes its nice service of worship with candles, flowers, and a somewhat chastened preacher. That is exactly what happened all over seventeenth-century England as the infamous and often obnoxious George Fox disrupted staid and orderly Anglican services with his message of spiritual inwardness and social equality. And the people called Quakers began.

This inner religion which Fox proclaimed to the churches seems to have haunted him from his earliest days. Born in 1624, he was a serious child, disgusted with the spiritual insensitivity of his elders. He wrote: "In my very young years, I had a gravity and staidness of mind and spirit not usual in children. When I came to eleven years of age, I knew pureness and righteousness, for while a child I was taught how to be kept pure."[3]

Other youth and "rude people" ridiculed his sober ways, but Fox ignored them. His religious concerns became increasingly intense until, in his nineteenth year, he experienced a time of spiritual upheaval. He was depressed, unable to sleep, torn with despair, and plagued by temptation. He suffered frequent attacks of blindness, demonstrating mental and spiritual disorder.

Fox sought the advice of various clergy, but their suggestions were somewhat less than helpful. One advised him to take tobacco and sing Psalms as a remedy for his state of mind. Another suggested that he needed to marry as a cure for his nervous disorder. One tried to bleed him with leeches and still another flew into a rage when Fox, on the way to be counseled, accidentally stepped on the reverend's carefully cultivated flower garden. "Empty, hollow casks," he called them, convinced that not only was the world filled with wickedness, but the priests had no answers to its sinful dilemma. "I thought them miserable comforters, and saw they were all as nothing to me, for they could not reach my condition," he said.[4]

Fox fasted, sought solitude, and mourned his sinfulness in what some would call the "dark night of the soul." He wrote: "When I myself was in the deep, shut up under all, I could not believe that I should ever overcome; my troubles, my sorrows, and my temptations were so great that I thought many times I should have despaired, I was so tempted."[5]

Gradually the nervous strains began to subside and Fox received "openings" which brought a new sense of the presence of God and an increasing number of divine revelations. He became convinced that education at Oxford or Cambridge was not what qualified one for ministry. The truth of God was discovered in the heart, not in temples or universities.

Finally, at age twenty-three, Fox experienced a flood of light which he described in this way: "When all my hopes in them [the clergy] and in all men were gone, so that I had nothing outwardly to help me, nor could I tell what to do, then, oh, then, I heard a voice which said, 'there is one, even Christ Jesus, that can speak to thy condition'; and when I heard it my heart did leap for joy."[6] He had discovered the gift of new life.

The succeeding days and months were filled with additional revelations. The Christ of history and creed had become a living, inner presence. Fox's own personality became a meeting place for the human spirit and the divine life. Sometimes he calls this spiritual quality the "inner light," "the seed," or "Christ within." But, whatever the term, he means the real, spiritual life which begins as an individual becomes aware of Christ and sets out to obey him.[7] This light within was present in every individual—pagan or Christian, Protestant or Catholic. It had but to be awakened as one recognized and accepted its presence.

It was in an effort to awaken the inner light in others that George Fox began preaching. He went forth with a message of immediate experience with Christ. He preached on hillsides and in marketplaces, in barns and prisons. Indeed, prison seemed his almost constant pulpit. He was jailed eight times for a total of some six years in prison. His first arrests came because of his nasty habit of interrupting the sedate church services by zealously and impatiently arguing with the minister in the midst of the morning sermon. Likewise, Fox and those who followed him refused to swear oaths in court or to remove their hats before their social betters. They used the informal "thee" instead of the formal "you" with all persons regardless of social status.

Fox's preaching in prison was so powerful that after his first imprisonment a sheriff, his wife and children became "friends" as Fox called those who were awakened to light within. But jailers were not always converted. One jailer struck him with a club and Fox says, "While he struck me I was moved in the Lord's power to sing and that made him rage the more."[8] He was kept for a time in the notorious Doomsday Prison where the grime and filth on the cell floor covered the tops of his boots, and when he sang hymns, the jailer poured the excrement of other prisoners on his head.

If jails failed, mobs tried to stop him. Once he was attacked by a mob which beat him with hands, sticks, and copies of the Bible, put him in stocks and chains, whipped him, and finally stoned him out of town.[9] Persecution brought him before judges and supposedly produced the popular name for the Friends of Truth as Fox advised one magistrate that he had best "quake" before the judgment of the Lord.

These Friends of God increased even in the midst of persecution, and in 1652 Fox went to Swarthmore Hall and there met Judge Fell and his wife Margaret. Margaret was profoundly touched by Fox's preaching and in tears cried out: "We are all thieves. We have taken the words of Scripture, but we know none of their truths in ourselves."[10]

The Fells gave aid and comfort to the new movement and eighteen years later, long after the death of Judge Fell, George Fox married Margaret, not before he asked permission of his followers and Mrs. Fell's children. The two were married in the company of ninety-four Friends, and Fox promptly left on a preaching journey while Margaret Fell Fox was arrested and imprisoned. During twenty-one years of marriage, the couple spent barely five years together.

The societies grew and soon Friends had spread throughout Britain and the New World. In the first twenty years, thousands of Friends went to prison and three hundred died from execution or imprisonment.

As with other sermons in this series, I am not advocating that we all become Quakers or assume their theological and biblical interpretations. Perhaps through their faith and work we can discover some basic truths about the Word of God and the gospel life as we confront it together.

First, George Fox reminds us of the importance of the inner light for understanding our relationship with God and one another. From John's gospel Fox read and proclaimed that the light of God has come to all in Christ Jesus. It is light which enlightens every man and woman, light which shines in the darkness and cannot be extinguished, light which, when discovered and lived out, shines through the Christian as light for all the world.

This discovery of the light within made a difference in the way early Quakers responded to persons. The extreme Calvinists of the seventeenth century suggested that no one possessed even a trace of God's grace and light. God bestowed his grace only on a few, the elect, whom he had chosen in his sovereignty. All others remained totally depraved, incapable of acts of saving goodness. They had no ray of light within and were blinded forever by satanic darkness.

Instead of beginning with darkness and evil, Fox began with light and God. The incarnation, the enfleshing of the Christ of God, had brought light to all persons. "As in Adam all die, in Christ are all made alive," Paul had proclaimed. In some the light shined forth as awakened by the

Spirit; in others it lay dormant, waiting to be awakened. Evil was serious and deadly and Fox attacked it mercilessly, but it was not more powerful than good.

Practically speaking, however, Fox's view of human nature meant that he treated public sinners very differently than did most of the religious folk of his day. He took the gospel to the most depraved of persons, believing that the light of Christ was ready to break forth in them. Was that naive? Perhaps. But it was what he saw in Jesus as documented in the Gospels. Jesus was ever reaching out to the tax collectors and public sinners, loving those whom *his* world had dismissed as incapable of being loved or chosen by God.

Many in today's church seem quite comfortable with drawing easy lines between the depraved and the elect, quick to use such easy distinctions as saved/lost, saint/sinner, pure/defiled, chosen/rejected. The use of such glib categories may well foster spiritual pride and exclusiveness. It may turn us away from persons, not toward them. Such a view often suggests that people really are not worth much unless they have religion like we have religion.

Others among us sometimes practice a more subtle, secular view of total depravity which categorizes persons in terms of "our kind" of people *versus* "those kinds" of people. It distinguishes between economic class and social status, labeling people as rich/poor, beautiful/ugly, crude/sophisticated, or intellectual/ignorant. Only those with comparable background or breeding are worthy of our care and friendship.

If Fox is right and all carry the light of God within, recognized or not, then it should make a difference in the way we treat all persons. You and I categorize others too easily. We often demand some social, moral, or theological conformity before we can love people. Jesus and George Fox loved persons as they were and trusted God to bring the light.

And if every individual carries something of God's light within, then each can be touched by God's love. Hope can come to the most hopeless of persons. If the light is present, though hidden, ignored or repudiated, there is still hope for murderers, thieves, prostitutes, and even the more sophisticatedly cruel. When there is no hope, no light, in the worst among us, there is no hope for any. Many of us need to see God's light hidden in some black men and women who turn to crime in their frustration with the poverty and dehumanization which surround them. Others of us need to see that light hidden in some white men and women who wear robes and hoods and burn crosses as a misguided way of responding to their own hatred and frustrations with life. If the light of God cannot come to black militant or white racist, how can it come to more "respectable" sinners?

Does this mean that we fail to take sin seriously? That we sentimentalize love and inhumanity, refusing to stand against evil? No, it means we acknowledge and oppose sin but take goodness more seriously than we do evil. It means that we learn to hope that love is indeed stronger than hate and that even the most hopeless individuals can be changed by the light of Christ within.

Second, the Quakers took that gospel of hope into the horrible places of their world with the faith that they could awaken the light even in those who seemed the most depraved. They read the twenty-fifth chapter of Matthew and concluded that the light of Christ was found in the hungry, that Christ the light shined in the imprisoned, and that Christ the light was cold and naked with the suffering of the world. It was not a matter of saying to the poor, the sinful, and the riffraff of the world, "Clean yourselves up and get like all the rest of us and then we will love you." Rather, the Quakers proclaimed, "Let us stand with you and care for you that the light of God's love may shine through us all."

For the true light enlightens every person. God has no favorites. None can be called common or unclean. In Christ Jesus there is no distinction in Jew and Greek, slave or free, male or female. Thus the Quakers recognized all spiritual gifts as exercised by both men and women. If God sets a person on fire, they said, he or she will awaken others and that, not ordination or sexual distinction, determines the true Christian calling. The worst of sins is to retard the light of God as it comes through any human being, male or female.

Wherever they found oppression and degradation, the Quakers attacked it. They supported a living wage for exploited workers and penal reform for the deplorable English prison system. They were early opponents of slavery and fearless enemies of war.

Finally, wherever they went, to rich or poor, oppressor or oppressed, the Quakers listened. For if everyone held the light of God, there was something to be learned from every human being. One Friend writes: "Mission is not message, but meeting, not preaching but encounter, in which listening is as much an act of love as speaking."

You and I desperately need to learn how to listen to one another. We talk at people, speaking without communicating, hearing without listening, pontificating as if we alone have light and others may receive it only from ourselves. How long since we really listened to spouses and parents, children and friends? How long since we took time to listen to the plight of hurting, lonely people before applying some all-too-easy response? How long since we really listened to God?

Fox looked with prophetic disgust upon the churches of his day with their elaborate symbols, their ornate sanctuaries, and their intricate formulas for bringing the grace of God to ordinary sinners. He declared that the symbols were too often the end instead of the means to true worship. Services might be filled with pious signs, symbols, songs, and sermons, but if they did not lead beyond themselves to God they were of no avail in the spiritual life. God was not trapped in the *Book of Common Prayer* or even in the Bible. He was not locked behind the stained glass of a church building, nor was knowledge of him given only to the clergy. God has visited his people, not just in the New Testament, but now. The church was called beyond symbolism without Spirit, routine without heart, and clericalism without pastoral care, to the dynamic reality of the living Christ.

Thus Fox turned to silence, not mere absence of words, but "the silence of personal search." To sit quietly and do nothing, subject to no pressures or coercion save thoughts of God and others, that was the heart of Quaker worship. God was everywhere with his people and nothing they could do in worship would make him more present. The early Quaker meetings began and ended with a sense of the immediate, intimate presence of God. If God is present, why not be still and know him as God? Silence did not guarantee experience with God. It was a means toward that experience which had to be learned and cultivated in the individual life.

And that is Fox's teaching for us: that God is first and foremost Spirit and the true worshipers are those who accept his presence in Spirit and truth. We do not need to tear down our churches, burn the choir robes, extinguish the candles, or destroy the organ. But we must recover the art of listening for the still small voice of God. We must rediscover the God who is behind our symbols, develop new symbols which speak to our own day, and learn the value of being silent before the Lord.

For we are the "Muzak" generation, surrounded by sound everywhere we go. Silence has become frightening for many of us. Each of us needs moments, even hours, of solitude and silence which permit us to think, reflect, and focus our attention on the presence of God in all facets of life.

We are a people grown all too familiar and comfortable with the noise pollution of our day and we pipe sound all about us. When we worship, we bombard ourselves with sound so that even our prayers are volleys of petition hurriedly spoken and hastily abandoned. Silence must be cultivated in worship and in our private lives. "Be still and know that I am God," the God who can come to us in the still small voice. Silence in the presence of God helps to transform us into whole persons thoughtfully moving beyond the frenzied pace of life, "centering down" toward the peace of God which strengthens us for life in the world.

What is the word which George Fox brings to us today? It is that we must learn to listen, to listen for the light. That sounds very strange at first, for we really do not hear light. We see it, or feel its warmth. Yes, but we must also learn to listen for it. Light is hope. Light is word, the word of God coming to us. Sometimes when the darkness of pain, loneliness, and sin is all around us we can see no light. But somewhere, deep within ourselves, our enemies, and our friends, we can hear the light of God's still small voice. Sometimes in the babbling sounds of our worship, our world, or our words, we hear no sounds of hope and truth. That is when we listen for the light. Listen, learn, wait, seek, and hear. Hear the light which is beyond words or understanding. Hear the light beyond words of hatred and cursing, anger, resentment, and despair. Hear the light even when you cannot see it or feel it. Believe that in every human being there is light and hope.

In our sin, in our guilt, in our moments of deepest need comes the Word of God: "The light shined in the darkness and the darkness could not put it out."

Listen. . . . The light is shining in your darkness. Can you hear it?

Notes

1. George Fox, *The Journal of George Fox*, edited with introduction by Rufus M. Jones (New York: Capricorn Books, 1963), pp. 92-93. I have

adapted this quote somewhat from Fox's own words. The introduction written by Rufus Jones provides a helpful outline for the sermon.

2. Ibid., p. 136.

3. Ibid., p. 66.

4. Ibid., p. 73.

5. Ibid., p. 83.

6. Ibid., p. 82.

7. Ibid., p. 33, and Rachel Hadley King, *George Fox and the Light Within* (Philadelphia: Friends Bookstore, 1940), p. 49.

8. Ibid., p. 191.

9. Ibid., p. 114.

10. Rufus M. Jones, *George Fox, Seeker and Friend* (New York: Harper and Brothers, 1930), p. 82.

Selected Bibliography

BARBOUR, HUGH. *The Quakers in Puritan England.* New Haven: Yale University Press, 1964.

FOX, GEORGE. *The Journal of George Fox.* New York: Capricorn Books, 1963.

JONES, RUFUS M. *George Fox, Seeker and Friend.* New York: Harper and Brothers, 1930.

KING, RACHEL HADLEY. *George Fox and the Light Within.* Philadelphia: Friends Bookstore, 1940.

NOBLE, VERNON. *The Man in Leather Breeches.* New York: Philosophical Library, 1953.

6.
John Wesley:
The Change Which God Works
2 Corinthians 5:16-21

If anyone is in Christ, he is a new creation; the old has passed away, behold, the new has come.

Perhaps John Wesley's story really begins, not with his birth in 1703, but six years later when he was trapped in the flaming rectory of the Anglican church in the village of Epworth. On that evening his father, the Reverend Samuel Wesley, gave his son up for lost and knelt in front of the burning house to commit the boy's soul to God. His daring and resourceful mother, Susanna, able to leap tall buildings in a single bound, was more active in her faith. With the help of neighbors she rescued the boy as "a brand plucked from the burning." Both father and mother believed that God had spared their son for some great mission.

John's father was a poetic man who had little head for practical matters of financial or family problems. He was rather unpopular with his parishioners due to his friendship with the local tax collector, his insistence on strict discipline, and his careful inquiry into the private lives of his church members. He was continually in debt, even spending time in prison for failure to pay his bills. Through it all, there was the guiding spirit of Susanna Wesley, one of the most remarkable women in Christian history. While her husband disciplined his flock, she gave birth to their nineteen children, instructed them to cry softly, and fear the rod. Susanna taught each child the Lord's Prayer by the time he or she could speak, and by age five each could read, spending six hours daily in the school she conducted in her home. She even wrote a theology textbook for her daughters.

At age seventeen John set out for Oxford, spending his student days rather typically, with much time given to tennis and water sports. He wrote home to ask for money and inform his mother of the racy gossip from university life. At Oxford he joined a group formed by his brother Charles for serious religious devotion. Their practice of constant attendance at worship, regular hours of private prayer, visitation of the sick, and a strict moral code earned them such names of ridicule as the "Holy Club," the "Godly Club," or the "Bible Moths." But their methodical system of organization and study produced the name Methodist, a name later applied to Wesley's followers. Through the influence of the Holy Club, Wesley decided to become an Anglican priest, receiving ordination in 1725.

In 1735 there came a challenge which Wesley's romantic nature could not refuse—the opportunity to serve as missionary to the new colony of Georgia. He went as pastor to the settlers and missionary to the Indians, writing that his chief motive for going was to save his own soul. He was under the sad delusion that one could be saved better in Georgia, of all places, than in England.

The trip over was characterized by violent storms, during which Wesley made a significant observation. The English passengers were terrified during each storm, but a group of German pietists (Moravians) on board were undaunted, singing hymns in the midst of the tumult. Wesley questioned one: "Were you afraid?" "I thank God, no," was the reply. "But were your women and children afraid?" "No, our women and children are not afraid to die."[1] John Wesley knew that he could make no such confession. In Georgia he met another pietist, August Spangenberg, who asked, "Do you know Jesus Christ?" Wesley responded, "I know He is savior of the world." Spangenberg continued, "True, but do you know he has saved you?" Wesley: "I hope he has died to save me." "Do you know it for yourself?" Spangenberg enquired. "I do," Wesley replied, confessing later that his answer was little more than vain words.[2] Again he realized that while he had strong religious convictions he had no inner assurance of salvation.

The land to which Wesley came was truly Georgia the unspoiled, but not so with Wesley's ministry. The work with the Indians was not as easy as he expected. They were not waiting like innocent children for the gift of the white man's gospel. The work with the Anglicans was little better. His religious rigorism alienated many parishioners.

And then there was the matter of romance. At age thirty-two he met Sophy Hopkey, a girl of eighteen, whom he taught French and spiritual instruction. He made plain his love for her but without formal declaration. Two friends persuaded him that it was not God's will, casting lots as final proof. Miss Sophy became engaged to another. Shortly thereafter, Wesley publicly humiliated her by refusing to give her communion. The scorned woman and her family brought formal charges, and Wesley decided that the Lord was calling him back to England. Georgia was a disaster.

He wrote: "I went to America to convert the Indian; but oh! who shall convert me?"[3] At home he met another pietist who listened to his spiritual travail and advised: "Preach faith till you have it; and then, because you have it, you will preach faith."[4] Good advice, but still he had no real assurance of his salvation. Charles Wesley had such an experience in May 1738, and John was more than ready. The events of May 24, 1738, are some of the most famous of Christian history. In the afternoon he went to Saint Paul's Cathedral where the choir sang the words of Psalm 130: "Out of the depths I cry unto thee." His travail continued. "In the evening," he writes,

I went very unwillingly to a society in Aldersgate Street where one was reading Luther's preface to the Epistle of the Romans. About a quarter before nine, while he was describing *the change which God works in the heart through faith* in Christ, I felt my heart strangely warmed. I felt I did trust Christ, Christ alone for salvation; and an assurance was given me that He had taken away my sins, even mine and saved me from the law of sin and death.[5]

It was a new beginning.

This change which God worked turned Wesley into a zealous preacher. He began to organize societies within the Church of England composed of individuals of like-minded evangelical conviction who "desire to flee from the wrath to come, to be saved from their sins."[6] As the work spread Wesley began an itinerant ministry which would long characterize the circuit riders of Methodism. Thus for nearly fifty years he traveled four to five thousand miles a year, most of it on horseback. It is estimated that in fifty years he preached over forty thousand sermons. Always he followed the words of his life's motto: "The world is my parish."

Wesley's message was clear: Christ has paid the price for our redemption. We can experience complete assurance of pardon and restored fellowship with God. Christ has not died for some select minority as the Calvinists suggested or for some economic and social elite as the Anglicans implied. God was in Christ reconciling the world to himself. It is a change which God desires to work in every human heart.

From Paul through Wesley the divine word comes to us. To those whose guilt keeps them from a word of forgiveness, whose cynicism keeps them from a gift of grace, whose legalism keeps them from a moment of joy, or whose loneliness keeps them from a sense of acceptance, comes the good news. You are reconciled to God, to one another, and to yourself in Christ Jesus. You and I are made one with "the goodness of God." In Christ we discover that we are loved, that we belong, and have been accepted into a new community.

Wesley believed what many of us often act as if we do not believe. People really do need Jesus Christ, and the experience of his grace truly does transform a human life. Wesley's word to so many modern Christians is that we do not have to be ashamed to share our faith. Nor do we need to be shackled to one particular style of evangelical witness. Many of us grew up with a superficial, impersonal evangelism promoted as the only way to be evangelical. It provided searching people with glib answers and superficial solutions, often with little concern for deeper involvement in the complex cares and struggles of human beings. It suggested that grace was a spiritual "quick fix," with little need for repentance or discipleship. We may reject that particular form of evangelism but we must never reject our calling to share the vital reality of faith in Christ with others.

People are broken, sinful, and hurting. All persons need the grace of God desperately. Grace is no superficial solution to the guilt, sin, and loneliness of the world but a way of hope in the midst of the hurts and horrors of life. Faith in Christ can change the human heart. We do not keep that faith to ourselves but offer it as best we can with integrity and personal concern for others.

Biblical evangelism involves sharing Christ in the context of varied human relationships and involvement in human suffering. Wesley knew that, believed it, and preached it long before the experience at Aldersgate. Yet somehow on that particular night he received that word for himself as never before. For John Wesley that was good news and so it is for us. We can proclaim unashamedly that God can change our hearts. Whether in gentle nurture or traumatic encounter, in blessed assurance or unexpected response, faith must be internalized and lived out as we become agents of God's reconciliation. The message which Wesley proclaimed was one of reconciliation with God.

Wesley also introduced a new method for proclaiming the change which God works in the heart. He moved out or was thrown out of the sedate and aristocratic Anglican churches of his day and "consented to be more vile," proclaiming the gospel in highways and hedges. "Field preaching," it was called, standing in English meadows and markets, on hillsides and in city squares with a gospel to and for the disenfranchised whom the "decent people" had written off as incapable of moral transformation or spiritual experience. His message was simple and direct: "I want thee for my Lord! I challenge thee for a child of God by faith. The Lord hath need of thee. Thou who feelest thou art fit only for hell, art just fit to advance his glory—the glory of his free grace. Believe in the Lord Jesus Christ and thou, even thou, art reconciled to God."[7]

Many from the poor and working classes believed and were changed. Wesley scandalized Anglicans by recruiting his first lay preachers from the lower classes. Infamous scalawags became new creations. John Nelson was one of these lay preachers, an artisan, who wrote of the first time he heard Wesley preach: "It made my heart beat like the pendulum of a clock and when he did speak, I thought his whole discourse was aimed at me. When he had done, I said, 'This man can tell the secrets of my heart.' "[8]

The method of open-air preaching and the call for dramatic conversion was the vehicle for Wesley's biblical, Christ-centered preaching. It was a method utilized and elaborated upon by later revivalists of the nineteenth and twentieth centuries in England and America. But the question which confronts our churches today is whether we have much of the method but less of the message. Wesley brought a word of new life to people outside the tradition-bound churches of his day. His message was that of the Bible, the evangelistic heart religion of New Testament Christianity. In our own day we have a variety of persons who claim to be evangelical. Many of them use elaborate methods but sometimes display a questionable message of easy belief and worldly success.

Wesley's method was a response to the Anglican obsession with form and order in religion. God, they implied, can best come to us in church buildings with choirs and clergy, dignity and order. Yes, said Wesley,

God can come in that ordered setting but he must also be shared with those outside the churches, the outcasts, the poor, the indifferent, and the criminal. So he went into the fields and established an informal type of evangelical preaching which became the norm for many groups to this day. Now, however, many in our churches believe that God only comes in the spontaneous and the informal. We contrive spontaneity and institutionalize informality, creating an evangelism with much style but often little substance. The grace gets a little cheaper and the cost of discipleship a little less costly and the promises of material success a little bolder. Instead of growth, change, or struggle with new truths and old sins we get a gospel of transaction. Pray a prayer and sign a card; no muss, no fuss. No need to grow, just get your doctrines straight. No need to question, we have all the answers. Wesley would have said to his day that it is possible to be an Anglican bishop without being religious and to our day that it is possible to be a Baptist evangelist without being evangelical.

The style of our worship—formal or folksy—does not guarantee the presence of God. Rather God is discovered in cathedrals, revivals, house churches, and Sunday School classes by faith, as people humbly seek to experience the God who breaks down our preconceived notions as to how, when, and where God may speak to us.

Perhaps Southern Baptists need a new Wesley or two who will bring prophetic judgment upon our obsession with particular forms of evangelism and lead us to a recovery of the good news of becoming new creations in Christ, however that may be expressed. We must rediscover an evangelism based in the Scripture and not necessarily shackled to the revivalistic techniques of the nineteenth and twentieth centuries. For discipleship and witness are inseparable. It is not just the way we talk or smile but the way we treat others, care for persons, and exercise the stewardship of our lives.

There is one other word which Wesley brings to us. He insisted that the change which God works in the heart never ends. Yes, the old life is over and a new life has already begun, but it is only a beginning. Aldersgate was but one of many experiences of new spiritual insight. After Aldersgate, Wesley then had to seek God as thoroughly by grace through faith as he had earlier done through the law. Faith was indeed a process. Had he "stopped there," one scholar writes, "the experience of Aldersgate would not have lasted through the night."[9]

The change which God works is continuous. God is ever making us new creations. The life of the gospel is a journey. It is not one prayer, one commitment, and we are fixed for life, as if we sign some heavenly contract and forget about it. In our emphasis on eternal security we Baptists have often led people to think little of becoming, growing, and maturing in Christ. Often we believe that once we have "walked the aisle" it is all over. No, it is only the beginning.

No one ever arrives; no one ever has all the truth of God. No one ever possesses or is possessed by the full gospel. That can lead only to pride and arrogance. We are always on the way. Never arrived, always arriving. Conversion is both event and process. I am converted but I am also being converted. That is the paradox of the gospel life. The new and the old creation exist together. That is at once the frustration and adventure of the life to which we have been called.

Wesley knew the enduring quality of the old creation throughout his life. He was frequently dictatorial, argumentative, petty, and egocentric. His married life was one constant source of insensitivity and antagonism. At forty-five he was nursed to health by a thirty-two-year-old widow, Grace Murray. Wesley told her he intended that they should marry. She would not wait forever and became engaged to another; John protested and she broke the engagement. John told brother Charles Wesley of his plans and Charles was convinced it was not God's will. He encouraged Grace to marry her original suitor. Foiled again!

At forty-eight he was nursed by another widow, kept his love a secret from Charles and married Molly Vazeille. He told her, "Be content to be a private insignificant person, known and loved by God and me . . . leave me to be governed by God and conscience. Then I shall govern you with gentle sway, and shew that I do indeed love you even as Christ the church."[10]

She was not content. It was a miserable marriage with three separations. The final break saw her carry private documents to his critics to be used against him. When she died, Wesley did not hear of it until several days after her burial.

In marriage all things had not become new, but he did not forsake the gospel life. The year before his death he wrote, "I am now an old man, decayed from head to foot. My eyes are dim; my right hand shakes much, my mouth is hot and dry every morning; I have a lingering fever almost every day; my motion is weak and slow. However, blessed be

God, I do not slack my labor. I can preach and write still."[11] He was dead at the age of eighty-seven leaving behind him, one has said, "nothing but a good library of books, a well-worn clergyman's gown, a much abused reputation, and the Methodist church."

Wesley's word of reconciliation still comes to us in the great Methodist hymns. Charles wrote the best words but the message was clearly John's.

> Soar we now where Christ has led,
> Following our exalted head,
> Made like him, like him we rise,
> Ours the cross, the grave, the skies.

John Wesley was right, God can change our hearts. Hallelujah!

Notes

1. *The Journal of John Wesley* (Chicago: Moody Press, 1952), p. 36.

2. Ibid., pp. 36-37.   3. Ibid., p. 53.   4. Ibid., p. 58.

5. Ibid., pp. 63-64.

6. Umphrey Lee, *The Lord's Horseman* (New York: The Century Co., 1928), p. 127.

7. John Wesley, "Justification by Faith," in Albert C. Outler, ed., *John Wesley* (New York: Oxford University Press, 1964), p. 209.

8. John Pudney, *John Wesley and His World* (New York: Charles Scribner's Sons, 1978), p. 71.

9. Robert G. Tuttle, Jr., *John Wesley, His Life and Theology* (Grand Rapids: Zondervan Publishing House, 1978), p. 200.

10. Pudney, p. 101.   11. *Journal*, pp. 412-13.

Selected Bibliography

EDWARDS, MALDWYN. *The Astonishing Youth*. London: The Epworth Press, 1959.

LEE, UMPHREY. *The Lord's Horseman*. New York: The Century Co., 1928.

OUTLER, ALBERT, ed. *John Wesley*. New York: Oxford University Press, 1964.

PUDNEY, JOHN. *John Wesley and His World*. New York: Charles Scribner's Sons, 1978.

WESLEY, JOHN. *The Journal of John Wesley*. Chicago: Moody Press, 1952.

7.
The Shakers:
Celebration and Security
Acts 2:42-47

They devoted themselves to the apostles' teaching and fellowship, to the breaking of bread and the prayers.

In the summer of 1774, eight members of the United Society of Believers in Christ's Second Appearing appeared in New York after a journey from England with their spiritual leader Ann Lee. If anyone took notice of them at all, it was as a band af religious fanatics whose theology was suited only for the lunatic fringe of the church. Today we call them Shakers and know them for the austere beauty of their crafts, the simplicity of their communal life, and the haunting plainsong of their worship. Indeed that the Shakers should have been rediscovered and appreciated by contemporary society is particularly ironic, for they are dying out. The society has been closed to new members since the 1960s and, after enduring for over two centuries, fewer than ten Shakers remain.

That is one reason why I have included them in this series of sermons. For Catholics, Lutherans, Methodists, Quakers, and Baptists are all alive and reasonably well, certainly not terminally ill. Soon the once thriving Shakers will be only a memory, studied by historians and sociologists, their communities made museums, their furniture sought, stolen, and copied.

Shaker theology seems very far from "mainline" Protestant groups discussed in other of these sermons. Their views regarding Mother Ann, the second coming, spiritualism, and revelation will not be acceptable to most modern Christians. But that does not negate other important truths which the Shakers taught and which the church has often overlooked.

What happens when a church loses hope, when nothing works any more, and the dream has failed? Can the Shakers speak one more time to the twentieth-century American church obsessed with success, numbers, and increasing assets? Can they provide a prophetic word to those who treat them with patronizing curiosity, a colorful but obsolete anachronism of American religion?

As the church confronts the latter days of the twentieth century, the Shakers bring an old message to us. They suggest that the ground of the church's life is found in two basic qualities: celebration and security.[1] None of us will decide to become Shakers, we could not if we wanted to, but that does not mean that we cannot learn from them and their unique expression of the gospel.

Before it ended, however, it began in the strange and tormented life of Ann Lee. Born in England in 1736, she was a serious, pious, and illiterate woman subject to visions which persuaded her of the total depravity of the human condition. Her morose spiritual state was compounded by the loss of four children in infancy, convincing her that human sexual relationships were evil and the cause of all sin. After months of anguish, she concluded that only by faith in Christ and acceptance of the "yoke" of celibacy could she experience the new birth.

She joined a charismatic group of "shaking Quakers" and soon the members were insisting that "Mother Ann" had a unique relationship with God. Just as God had revealed himself in Jesus, so he was speaking in a special way through this woman. Persecution increased with these new revelations and soon the little band departed for America, arriving in 1774, prepared to establish the initial stages of the kingdom of God on earth.

Settling near what is now Albany, New York, the Shakers soon sent missionaries to New England and despite severe persecution from the Puritans, Shaker communities sprang up in Massachusetts, Maine, Connecticut, and New Hampshire. Mother Ann led in these missions and the harsh treatment which she received from unbelievers hastened her death in 1784. But some had responded positively and before long Shaker doctrines spread, particularly through the influence of the religious awakenings which swept colonial America.

The Shakers demanded a radical response to the gospel from those seeking to follow the newfound spiritual life of the revivals. By 1800 they moved west to frontier Ohio and Kentucky where revivals produced emotional outbursts and dramatic conversions. In the backwoods, Baptists and Methodists shouted, jumped, and shook like the Shakers. Thus Shaker missionaries found fertile ground as they preached their views to those whose religious enthusiasm was well suited for the demands and dynamics of Shaker life.

While their emotionalism might have been compatible with that of the frontier revivals, their theology was not. God, the Shakers said, was expressed in qualities both male and female, as evidenced in the lives of Jesus and Mother Ann. The Christ Spirit had spoken uniquely through both of them. Thus to enter a Shaker community new converts were required to confess their sins, profess faith in Christ, and accept the yoke of celibacy as taught by Mother Ann. "In the kingdom of heaven there is neither marrying nor giving in marriage," Jesus had said. In the new kingdom (Shaker communities) men and women lived in families as brothers and sisters, carefully segregated in the same house, ever under the watchful eyes of governing elders and eldresses.

They drew inspiration from the New Testament church, practicing a community of goods, holding all things in common, and giving themselves to prayer and worship, separated from the world in ordered communities. Through confession, worship, and community life, they sought freedom from sin and the pursuit of spiritual perfection. This concern for perfection was evident in all aspects of Shaker life. Whether in devotions or furniture-building, Mother Ann's words were a motto: "Put your hands to the work and your hearts to God. Work as though you will live a thousand years and as though you will die tomorrow."

And work they did. Up with first trumpet at 4:30 AM, kneeling in silent prayer where the foot first touched the floor. Each dressed with right arm first, stepped with right foot first, and walked on tiptoe to the workshop. Villages were immaculate. One visitor declared: "The paint is all fresh. The planks are bright clean . . . a sheen is on everything; a happy quiet reigns. Every building has the air of a chapel."[2]

They built simple, useful furniture, were known for their seeds and home remedies, and invented such things as the common clothes pin, a washing machine, and a reaping device. The concern was for simplicity, humility, and order. They ate little meat, drank no tea, coffee, or spirits, and were health-food freaks long before it became the fad.

Theirs was a rigorous life but not an unhappy one. One scholar writes: "The facts of Shaker craftsmanship alone deny unhappiness. No one who was frustrated, repressed, discontented, or ill adjusted to life could have produced such simple, eloquent work, which breathes the air of tranquility and fulfillment."[3]

Such was Shaker life, reaching its height in the 1850s with some six thousand adherents. Now they are almost gone, declining with the advent of the modern industrial age. Clearly they were one-sided in their rejection of marriage and their attitude toward human sexuality. Sometimes their way of life was too legalistic and their leaders too dictatorial. Their theology was questionable at certain points and they acknowledged that their monastic-like life was not for every person.

Yet, like all those discussed in this volume, the Shakers tell us something about the nature of Christ's church, a church bound together by celebration and security.

The Shakers call us to the book of Acts and the celebration of a new community beginning to discover the reality and presence of the resurrected Christ. There we find a new people meeting together to hear again the stories of Jesus' life, death, and resurrection. Together they learned to celebrate life, sometimes even to celebrate death, always to affirm the presence of God with his people.

Celebration is as old and as unpredictable as the biblical record. It is Sarah laughing at the angelic news that a geriatric should bear a child so long hoped for and almost forgotten. It is David dancing for joy because the ark of God's presence has been restored to his people. It is Jesus celebrating with a man and woman at their marriage feast, furnishing the best wine for their special occasion. It is Paul and Silas singing hymns in prison. It is the new community of the church rejoicing together in the breaking of bread and prayers. It is even the writer of Revelation composing hymns of hope as Christians are being martyred for their faith.

And it is the Shakers in New England, New York, and frontier Kentucky singing their simple songs, dancing their ordered steps, celebrating together as a community of praise and joy.

Their meetings began with a hymn, a brief sermon, and then celebration. Shakers wrote their own hymns, tunes, and accompanying exercises. Men and women moved in separate groups, shaking, whirling, trembling, stamping, and singing. It was the best show for miles around, and outsiders came for amusement and curiosity. But to the Shakers it was worship, free and full of adoration and celebration before the Lord. In their singing and dancing they became oblivious to their audience and focused all their attention toward the praise of God. Their most familiar hymn describes their sense of celebration.

> 'Tis the gift to be simple,
> 'Tis the gift to be free,
> 'Tis the gift to come down
> Where we ought to be.
> And when we find ourselves
> In the place just right,
> 'Twill be in the valley
> Of love and delight.

The church is ever seeking to express its joy through celebration. We are a very different group in a very different context from the Shakers but celebration is essential to community, and we often desperately need to discover the freedom of it. Sometimes we do not even know those seated next to us at worship in our anonymous congregations. Often in our diversity we do not see each other except on occasional Sundays. We inhabit diverse worlds—retired persons, students, teachers, families, singles—and communication can be difficult for us. As impersonal congregations we often say to the preacher, the choir, and the musicians, "All right, here we are, tickle our ears, entertain us, do something profound. Do not require us to become involved in this performance." But the worship celebration is for all of us. It is participated in, not observed. It is lived, not endured; anticipated, not dreaded. Joyful, yet somber, it is a sign of wholeness and humanity before God.

Celebration is not hilarity, frivolity, or blind enthusiasm. It is not positive thinking when the world is crashing in about us. Celebration in a real sense is the cry of a hurting and hoping people affirming that God is present when we do not feel him or want him or when we can make no sense out of life as it comes to us.

We must celebrate, not in superficial pep rallies where pain is ignored or stoically repudiated, not in some variety show entertainment which dulls us to the hurt about us and within us, not in a cool sophistication which refuses to become vulnerable to the struggles of others. What we celebrate is life in Christ, life together in the midst of struggle and sadness. Paul's profound confession in 2 Corinthians is something of what true celebration is all about. He writes:

Hard-pressed on every side, we are never hemmed in; bewildered, we are never at our wits end; hunted, we are never abandoned to our fate; struck down, we are not left to die. Wherever we go we carry death with us in our body, the death that Jesus died, that in this body also life may reveal itself, the life that Jesus lives (2 Cor. 4:8-10, NEB).

That is why we can know joy at funerals and sadness at births, why we as God's people are ever celebrating in the most unlikely places the simple love, goodness, and profundity of the human/divine relationship.

Where does celebration come from? "As deep a place as tears come from," says Frederick Buechner. Perhaps the same place.[4] It is Jesus crying out, even on the way to the cross, "Be of good cheer; I have overcome the world." The church, even through its tears, is a celebrating community. For if God is really with us, there is always ground for hope and celebration.

The Shakers call us to remember something else, that the church is to be a place of security. In the coarse, impersonal environment of the American frontier, to abused women and children, to slaves and social outcasts, to people afraid of life and without a place the Shakers gave the security of a beloved community. "Whatever your past may have been, confess your sins and begin anew," they said. "Share yourself and all you have, and all you need will be shared with you." Escape? Perhaps, but for many it was a sense of belonging which they had never known before.

Almost from the beginning, the New Testament writers described the security which the church provided for a new people. There they were, those early Christians, some having lost family because of their new faith, some having no family or earthly ties save those they found in the church. People who by circumstance or choice were cut off from their past now became a part of the new community of the church, receiving the security of right relationship with God, the security found in a community of forgiven, forgiving sinners. "Confess your faults to one another, and pray for one another." "Bear one another's burdens and so fulfill the law of Christ." In this community, Paul writes to the Colossians, kindness, humility, gentleness, patience, and forgiveness reign. The early church struggled with this as we do. Sometimes they were a community of paranoia, mistrust, and malice, not peace and security. Therefore, Paul taught: You are all one body, intimately related; when one weeps, all weep; when one rejoices, all rejoice.

The contemporary church must be a community where we are challenged and confronted with the gospel demand to become more than we ever dreamed we could be, where bearing the cross, sacrificing for others, weeping and laughing together are taken seriously as a part of Christian growth and maturity. Yet along with the trauma of growth and discipleship there is always the security of a family.

Sometimes life is so heavy upon us there is no way to celebrate. Sometimes there is no way out of pain, hurt, and death. At such times we need the security of the church, security which allows us to cry out and which holds on to us, loves us, and believes in us even when we do not believe in ourselves. Fall on your face, and no one will laugh. Cry out in unbelief, and no one will denounce you as faithless. Confess your sins and no one will condemn you in self-righteousness. The church is a place where you have the security to be insecure and the help to become whole.

That should mean much to us for we are the insecure generation desperately seeking to find out who we are, who we can become, and what life is about. Am I OK? Are you OK? Are we OK together? Is God OK at all? In everything from *Passages*[5] to Zen, est to drugs, alcohol to fundamentalism, our society seeks answers to its insecurities. And the church is often the center of such insecurities, prejudices, and jealousies. We Christians provide easy, armchair analyses of one another, sometimes with polite and subtle cruelty. "What she really needs. . . ." "What he ought to do. . . ." "The real reason he acts that way is. . . ." And we play a kind of ecclesiastical one-ups-person-ship on one another, diagnosing every weakness as if we had all the answers and could solve every problem. Or, we madly search for weakness in one another, not to bear common burdens, but to win in some piously diabolical game of spiritual "gotcha." However, when the church is really the body of Christ, we are free to confess our sins. By God's grace, we are secure enough to acknowledge weakness, appreciate strength, and begin again.

What then is the church? An organization of programs, procedures, and policies with bylaws for every problem? A storehouse of answers where doubt and failure can never be tolerated? Or a community celebrating even in struggle, providing the security of love even in the insecurity of life. Let us say to all who pass by, "Come and celebrate with us"; "Come and find security for yourself in our searching, helping, community." "Come put your hands to the work and your hearts to God." "But if you do not choose this way or if you do and then go elsewhere, those who remain will continue celebrating and caring for one another in Christ's name, working as if we would live a thousand years and as if we would die tomorrow."

And what about the handful of Shaker women who remain? What must they think of God? For when they joined the society as young women they surely thought that it would last forever, that community of celebration and security. But things did not go according to plans and the community to which they gave their lives will soon pass into extinction. What a waste, some will say, to spend your life in a dying cause.

And what of the modern church? What will we do when failure and decline, pain and disappointment descend? What then? Do we throw in the towel? Fight it out with each other, blame and criticize? Shake our angry fists at one another and at God? Or can we sing in celebration and security, in tears and hope, the hymn which a handful of Shaker sisters still sing in the early mornings at Sabbathday Lake, Maine.

> Lead me on to greater victory
> Bear me to the conqueror's throne,
> Let me sing the song triumphant,
> I the world have overcome.[6]

"After all," says one old Shaker saint who yet remains behind, "we do not lose hope. For the Spirit will make itself felt again, somewhere, somehow."[7] That is not only the hope of the Shakers, that is the hope of the church, hope which for all of us is truly the good news of God.

Notes

1. Marguerite Fellows Melcher, *The Shaker Adventure* (The Press of Western Reserve University, 1960), p. 5. Ms. Melcher suggests two abiding

qualities of Shaker life: adventure and security. I have modified those ideas with the emphasis on celebration and security as applied to the church in general.

2. Mark Holloway, *Heavens on Earth* (New York: Dover Publications, Inc., 1966), p. 70.

3. Ibid., p. 74.

4. Frederick Buechner, *Telling the Truth, The Gospel as Tragedy, Comedy and Fairy Tale* (New York: Harper and Row, 1977), p. 56.

5. Gail Sheehy, *Passages: Predictable Crises in Adult Life* (New York: E. P. Dutton, 1976).

6. C. Allyn Russell, "The Rise and Decline of the Shakers," *New York History* (January, 1968), p. 49.

7. Melcher, *The Shaker Adventure,* p. 285.

Selected Bibliography

ANDREWS, EDWARD DEMING. *The People Called Shakers.* New York: Dover Publications, Inc., 1953.

HOLLOWAY, MARK. *Heavens on Earth.* New York: Dover Publications, Inc., 1966.

MELCHER, MARGUERITE FELLOWS. *The Shaker Adventure.* The Press of Western Reserve University, 1960.

NORDHOFF, CHARLES. *Communistic Societies of the United States.* New York: Dover Publications, Inc., Reprint of 1875 edition, 1966.

8.
Sojourner Truth: Free at Last
Galatians 3:26 to 4:7

There is neither slave nor free . . . for you are all one in Christ Jesus.

Slavery, Lerone Bennett says, was a black man who stepped out of his African hut and ended up ten months later in Georgia with bruises on his back and a brand on his chest.[1] Slavery was belonging to a master—having no family and no name—sold anytime, anywhere. Slavery was a black man committing suicide in order to escape his bondage. Slavery was the child Isabella sold at auction as her parents, freed by the master's last will and testament, watched helplessly. It was Isabella herself, a generation later, watching as her own son, Peter, was sold and taken from her. And with that experience, the slave girl Isabella became a free woman with a new name, Sojourner Truth, and a new calling to tell slavery's story and abolish it forever.

Isabella, who became Sojourner Truth, was born in Ulster County, New York, probably in 1797. The birth date of slaves was seldom recorded. She was a slave in the North, born before slavery was abolished there, working on the large farms of Dutch immigrants in upstate New York almost from the time she could walk.

But slavery was more costly in the northern climate than in the South, and owners had to protect their assets carefully. Masters often freed slaves, not out of concern or conviction, but when they became too old to work or were of no resale value. Thus, when Isabella was eleven, her parents old and tired, were set free, but she was worth $150 and was sold at action, carried off from her parents, alone and afraid, to be sold again and again. One, two, three hundred dollars for a human being. The ads frequently read, "A sturdy black wench able to work hard and bear children."

She grew tall and talkative and became a favored slave. "Master's pet," the others called her, patronized by whites, ridiculed and mistrusted by blacks. Having no people, she moved from master to master, from fields to kitchen, working from dawn to dark, waiting for freedom. In 1817 the Freedom Law was passed in New York. It called for the emancipation, the gradual emancipation, of all slaves after a ten-year interim. The blacks heard the news: "You are free . . . but not for 10 years." Imagine, after all those years, freedom . . . but not yet. Suppose you died in eight or nine years, dying days or months from freedom; so near to it and yet not free.

Two years from Freedom Day the master sold Isabella's son, Peter. He was only four years old but the master needed the money. "Oh, master it's only two years to freedom," she pleaded. But Peter was young, money was scarce, and he had to be sold. A year later Isabella could stand no more of it. She claimed freedom for herself and fled, hidden and befriended by Quakers. She was free at last until her master found her and returned her to slavery.

In the days after her capture, she turned beyond herself and her world of despair to the religion of Jesus and it became the compelling force in her life. It came dramatically in her depression, whether a voice or an unseen presence, she was never really sure. This is how she described it:

I began to feel it was somebody that loved me and I tried to know him." And I said, "I know you! I know you! I know you! . . ." And when I said, "I know you, I know you," the light came. . . . And finally something in me spoke up and said, "This is Jesus. Glory be to God!" And the whole world grew bright and the trees they waved and waved in glory and every little bit of stone on the ground shone like glass. And I shouted, "Praise, praise, praise the Lord." And I began to feel such a love in my soul as I never felt before—love to all creatures. . . . And I cried out loud, "Lord, Lord, I can love even the white folks. Jesus loves me. He'll love me always. I won't be lonely any more."[2]

But then came the fear, "If I let the white folks know about me and Jesus, maybe they'll get him away from me too." She could not risk it. "No one must know he had come to her."[3]

With time, freedom came, a new freedom and a new boldness. Freedom Day was July 4, 1827. Isabella and all New York slaves were set free. Immediately she went to court, sued the man who had taken her son, and regained custody of her boy with damages. She was learning. She too was a person. She received with sadness and joy the beaten whimpering and frightened boy who was her son. He did not even know she was his mother.

Some white folks invited her to church. She went hesitantly, still fearing they would try to take her Jesus away from her. But they knew him and loved him too, and she joined the Methodist Church.

Freedom took her to New York City where she worked cooking, cleaning, and caring for the sick. There she began to tell of her faith and her slavery, working with evangelical groups and street preachers in the Bowery among the poor. On street corners she would appear to sing in hushed tones a song of her own composing:

> It was early in the morning,
> It was early in the morning,
> just at the break of day,
> When he rose, when he rose, when he rose
> and went to heaven on a cloud.[4]

And as she began to sing and speak of her story, the ex-slave named Isabella discovered a new name and a new calling. One unexpected day in 1843, she felt the conviction that her old slave name was taken away and that God would give her a new one. It came quietly, that pilgrim name: Sojourner. Some ridiculed her name and her mission, so she demanded more. " 'Oh, God, give me a name with a handle on it.' And it came to me like a voice as true as God is true: Sojourner Truth—Truth shall be my abiding name till I die."[5]

Sojourner Truth traveled throughout the eastern states, singing to draw a crowd, telling the story of slavery and Jesus. Soon the abolitionists discovered her. They were wild-eyed young men and women, crying with prophetic determination against the sin of slavery. "Join us," they said, "and tell your story to the nation."

She joined them and soon the tall black figure with the deep voice was known across the North for her songs and her stories. Still she sang of the despair of her people.

> I am pleading for my people, a poor downtrodden race,
> who dwell in freedom's boasted land with no abiding place.
> While I bear upon my body the scars of many a gash,
> I am pleading for my people who groan beneath the lash.[6]

Her quick wit was soon known to those who crossed her. After speaking one day, Sojourner was accosted by a man who demanded: "Old woman, do you think your talk about slavery does any good? Do you suppose people care what you say? Why, I don't care any more for your talk than I do for the bite of a flea." "Perhaps not," she replied, "but the Lord willing, I'll keep you scratching."[7]

And in Ohio, where wheat crops were blighted by weevils, she recalled,

This morning I was talkin' to God in the wheat field. I saw the wheat lookin' so big. I goes up and takes hold of it and would you believe it? There was no wheat there. I says, "God, what ails this wheat?" He says, "Sojourner, there is a little weevil in it." Now I hears talk about the constitution and the rights of man. I comes up and takes hold of this constitution. It looks mighty big. I feels for my rights but they ain't there. Then I says, "God what ails the constitution," and he says, "Sojourner, there's a little weevil in it."[8]

Sometimes clergymen challenged her right to speak to men. Women were to keep silent. At one rally, confronted by many males, she shouted,

I could work as much and eat as much as any man and bear the lash as well and aren't I a woman? I have borne children and seen them sold into slavery and when I cried with a mother's grief, none but Jesus heard me. And aren't I a woman? Some say woman can't have as much rights as a man cause Christ wasn't a woman. Where did Christ come from? From God and a woman. Man had nothing to do with him. If the first woman God ever made was strong enough to turn the world upside down all alone, all women together ought to be able to turn it back and get it right side up again and now that they are asking to do it, the men better let 'em.[9]

The applause was deafening.

Time passed, the Civil War exploded and a nation strained beyond the breaking point. Through it all, Sojourner Truth traveled and fought for her people and her Lord. She fought segregation in the North on trains and in housing. At seventy-three someone asked her to write her biography. "No," she said, "I'm not ready to be writ up yet, for I still have lots to accomplish."[10]

Once on a segregated railroad car, she sat in the white section with a white woman companion. The conductor grabbed her and ordered her off. The white friend protested. "Does she belong to you?" the conductor demanded. "She belongs to humanity," Sojourner's friend replied. The conductor threw them both off the train. Sojurner Truth sued the railroad for assault and battery. The conductor was fired and Sojourner said that before the trial was over Northern railroad cars looked like "salt and pepper."[11] No injustice was left unchallenged.

She died at eighty-six with words of the old song on her lips:

> It was early in the morning,
> It was early in the morning,
> just at the break of day,
> When he rose, when he rose, when he rose
> and went to heaven in a cloud.[12]

Sojourner Truth and the slave experience testifies, Martin Marty has said, to the reality of hope in the midst of the tragedy of life; that hope is a real and powerful force when hopelessness seems rampant.[13] The slave experience seemed the ultimate in hopelessness. They were kidnapped or born into slavery, packed into slave ships, and sold at auction. They had no homes, no families, and were treated like animals, always subject to the whims of the master. There are no good masters when you are a slave.

Yet so many of them found hope—when there seemed no hope at all. Eugene Genovese, a Marxist and a historian, set out several years ago to describe the slave experience and prove that religion kept the blacks in bondage with false hope and promises of pie-in-the-sky-by-and-by. What he found and writes about in the monumental volume *Roll, Jordan, Roll,* was that faith was often the only thing which gave slaves identity, humanity, and hope. It kept them believing till freedom came. They sang of that hope in the melodies of the slave experience. Of deliverance: "Didn't my Lord deliver Daniel, then why not every man?" Of justice: "O Mary, don't you weep, don't you moan, Pharaoh's army got drowned." Of pathos: "Nobody knows the trouble I've seen, nobody knows but Jesus."

The fact is that most of us middle class, Anglo-Saxon types do not often have to hope; we have all we need right now. We do not need to hope for freedom, we receive it by being born into our particular American social class. We do not need to hope for food, family, or homes, we have all that right now. We do not need to hope for justice—we have the money to hire a lawyer (and hope for the best).

Suppose things go wrong for us. Suppose we lose freedom or possessions, health or homes? Suppose, having all those, we lose our will to live? What then? Can we learn that audacious and adventuresome faith which anticipates a new day and a way back from hopelessness?

It dawned on me recently how our ideas of heaven might relate to all this. I heard the words of the black spirituals: "Swing low, sweet chariot, comin' for to carry me home," and "I got a robe, you got a robe, when I get to heaven, gonna put on my robe," and I dismissed all that as a crutch, escapist religion, often a trick to keep slaves and other oppressed people docile in a miserable world. Gradually, however, I realized that many of us do not need heaven. We have heaven right here. We do not need to wait for a robe, we already have a closet full of clothes. We do not need to wait for shoes, we already have them on. Perhaps heaven is not all that necessary for us secure, happy American types.

But when there is not an ounce of hope, heaven can become an important reality, indeed, a necessity. When there seems no justice, when there appears to be no end to suffering, when life develops cracks, and our dreams and securities crumble, when wrong seems to win out over everything good, then the reality of heaven comes to us. No, I'm not absolutely sure if heaven has gates of pearl and streets of gold. I do not care if we get mansions, condominiums, or dormitories, or if there is standing room only. If at last somewhere there is justice and peace, restoration and love, and the all-encompassing presence of the living God, that is heaven enough for me. Sojourner herself was once asked: "Suppose there is no heaven. What will you say if you never get there?" In a twinkle she replied, "Why, I'll say, 'Bless the Lord!' I had a good time thinking I would!"[14]

Sometimes hope—heaven—is all we have in the tragic moments of life. Hope that all this love is not wasted; that all this goodness is not lost; that all this caring is not empty. For in the end there is God and wherever, whenever, and however it works, that is heaven enough. We can and must find hope in the midst of the tragic.

Marty reminds us of another word Sojourner and the black religious experience bring to us today: the sense of peoplehood. In the common experience of slavery, segregation, and hopelessness, a people was born—a people hoping, waiting, dreaming of freedom. James Baldwin described it as:

zest and a joy and a capacity for facing and surviving disaster that are very moving and very rare. . . . Perhaps we were all of us . . . bound together by the nature of our oppression, the specific and peculiar complex of risks we had to run; if so, within these limits we sometimes achieved with each other a freedom that was close to love. . . . We had each other and had no need to pretend to be what we were not. That is the freedom that one hears in some gospel songs . . . and in jazz. . . . Something tart and ironic, authoritative and double-edged.[15]

Tragedy and joy, shared together. They had nothing else but each other. They came together to worship and became one people, with one voice. The preachers spoke, but everybody answered. All responded with shouts, amens, and hallelujahs. They were a people like Israel, a people in bondage, a people waiting for de-liverance—**together.**

Don't you wish that all God's church could discover this sense of peoplehood beyond sect, creed, or dogma? Don't we share common identity based in uncommon event, the coming among us of Jesus the Christ and the response of a people to that event. We prefer, it seems, to remain fragmented, to speak only of *our* Christ, *our* Bible, *our* church, or *our* doctrines.

Could we hear, really hear for ourselves, the ancient words: "In Christ there is neither Jew or Greek, slave or free, male or female, young or old, permanent or transient, rich or poor, black or white"?

We have often used that verse from Galatians when we are on the outside wanting in. "Let us in," we demand. "Give us our rights—slaves, women, Gentiles, and outsiders—all must be included fully in the church." It means just that, but it also means that once in, we are all together in Christ, every one of us. It is not just one faction getting into Christ's church and remaining a faction. It is one faction, another, and another becoming one whole people in Christ Jesus. Diversity and uniqueness, yes, but in the fullest sense in God's church there are no factions, no outsiders or insiders, no halfway members. You are not less a member of the church because you have no formal theological education or less a member because you give less money or spend less time in church activities. We are one people, and we must struggle to cultivate a sense of peoplehood together.

Truth is that we spend much of our time using our Bibles to keep people out, not letting them in. One of the haunting realities of my life is the knowledge that if I had lived in the 1840s, 50s, or 60s, I might have stood in Christian pulpits and, using this Bible, defended human slavery on the basis of a "literal" interpretation of the Word of God. And if I might have defended slavery then, what with this same Bible am I defending now which dehumanizes persons and is an offense to the gospel of Christ?

Jesus means freedom and that is devastating for us. For it means we have to live as if we were subject to none and simultaneously subject to all, as if everything belonged to us and as if we were entitled to nothing. It is that dangerous, exciting freedom which allows us to become whole persons in community and in commitment to one another—a people together.

In a real sense we are all sojouners, you and I, pilgrims on the way together—a way which sometimes seems clear, but just as often turns cruel and uncertain, a way that leads to the cross and beyond it to resurrection. And as we walk, alone and together, let us sing with hope the words of a triumphant people:

> Free at last, free at last,
> Great God a-mighty, we are free at last.

Notes

1.Lerone Bennett, *Before the Mayflower* (Baltimore: Penguin Books, 1966), pp. 30-31.

2. Jacqueline Bernard, *Journey Toward Freedom, the Story of Sojourner Truth* (New York: W. W. Norton and Co., 1967), pp. 66-67.

3 Ibid., p. 67.

4. Arthur Huff Fauset, *Sojourner Truth: God's Faithful Pilgrim* (Chapel Hill: University of North Carolina Press, 1938), p. 123. The period in New York was an interesting and much more complicated era in her life than I have indicated here. Some readers may wish further information in available sources.

5. Ibid., pp. 110-111, and Bernard, *Journey Toward Freedom*, pp. 121-22.

6. Bernard, *Journey Toward Freedom*, p. 149.

7. Fauset, *Sojourner Truth*, p. 137.

8. Bernard, *Journey Toward Freedom*, p. 173.

9. Ibid., pp. 166-67, and Fauset, *Sojourner Truth,* pp. 132-33.
10. Ibid., p. 223.
11. Ibid., p. 216.
12. Fauset, *Sojourner Truth,* pp. 178-79.
13. Martin E. Marty, Gheens Lectures, delivered at Southern Baptist Theological Seminary, March 24, 1976.   I am indebted to Professor Marty for the initial insights on the nature of the black religious experience in America. I have elaborated here on his basic points.
14. Bernard, *Journey Toward Freedom,* pp. 251-52.
15. James Baldwin, *The Fire Next Time* (New York: Dell Publishing Co., 1964), pp. 59-60.

Selected Bibliography

BENNETT, LERONE. *Before the Mayflower.* Baltimore: Penguin Goods, 1966.

BERNARD, JACQUELINE. *Journey Toward Freedom, the Story of Sojourner Truth.* New York: W. W. Norton Company, 1967.

FAUSET, ARTHUR HUFF. *Sojourner Truth: God's Faithful Pilgrim.* Chapel Hill: University of North Carolina Press, 1938.

GENOVESE, EUGENE. *Roll, Jordan, Roll: The World the Slaves Made.* New York: Pantheon Books, 1974.

GILBERT, OLIVE, ed. *Narrative of Sojourner Truth.* Battle Creek, 1884.

PAULI, HERTHA. *Her Name Was Sojourner Truth.* New York: Appleton, Century, Crofts, Inc., 1962.

9.
Lottie Moon: Of No Reputation
Philippians 2:5-11

He humbled himself and became obedient unto death, even death on a cross.

She was one of the first women in the South to receive a Master of Arts degree. As a youth she was indifferent to religion and read with sympathy the works of Thomas Paine, one of America's first "secular humanists." Her religious consciousness was renewed in a college revival and she went to China as one of the first single women sent out by Southern Baptists. In China she fought for equality as a woman missionary, was accused by Baptist fundamentalists of failing to teach orthodox doctrine, and pledged to marry one of the most infamous "liberals" in Southern Baptist life. She refused to label the unconverted Chinese as "heathen" and died of malnutrition from sharing her meager fare with Chinese friends. A religious revolutionary? Perhaps, in her own unique way. A Southern Baptist institution? Absolutely.

Her name was Charlotte Digges Moon but to those who knew her and to those Baptists for whom she may well be the thirteenth apostle, she is Lottie, a name synonymous with the best of the church's missionary task in the modern era. It is difficult to preach about Lottie Moon and avoid the extremes by which such persons are often evaluated. For some she was the sainted, martyred missionary who seldom doubted and was always sure of her calling. Some see her as austere and self-sacrificing beyond measure, a holy person who gave up the gentility of a southern plantation for the wretchedness of "godless China." For others, Lottie Moon, like all our heroes, must be "demythologized" to prove that she was just as weak, conniving, sinful, and small-minded as the rest of us. Still others prefer to use her as a "proof text" for an ever-changing array of causes—feminism, new mission methods, pop religion—which "Miss Lottie" would surely support "if she were alive today."

Some recent studies of her life, particularly that by Catherine Allen, have sought to avoid those extremes and deal with Lottie Moon as a human being, given to great dreams and great disappointments, profound commitment, serious faults, and even common boredom. This sermon provides an all too brief account of her intriguing life and the Word of God which came to her.

Born in Virginia in December 1840, Lottie Moon "grew up" to stand 4 feet, 3 inches tall (or short, perhaps), spending her early life at Viewmont, the family plantation of several thousand acres and a large number of slaves. There were seven children in the household and the model of a strong-willed female was surely impressed upon them early when in 1853 their father, Edward Moon, was killed in a riverboat fire and their mother, Anna Maria Moon, assumed full responsibilities as "mistress" of Viewmont.[1] Indeed, the Moon children were apparently encouraged to think for themselves and pursue their interests in their own individual ways. Three became physicians including Orianna, Lottie's older sister, who went north for her education, becoming a feminist and an abolitionist sympathizer. After further study in Paris, she returned to the South to serve as a physician in Confederate Army hospitals. There she met and married another doctor, and the two practiced medicine together. Along the way, Orianna bore twelve sons.[2] Lottie was not the only Moon to live a unique and colorful life.

Like her sister, Lottie showed outstanding intellectual abilities, receiving her college education at the Albemarle Female Institute from which she graduated in 1861 with a Master's degree in the classics.[3] During this time, she experienced a renewal of her childhood faith and an increased concern for divine direction in her life. After the Civil War brought dissolution to the old way of life at Viewmont, Lottie became a teacher in schools in Alabama and Kentucky. In 1871, with Anna Cunningham Safford, she founded a female high school in Cartersville, Georgia. The school was something of a success but the two teachers were restless in their work. They talked of God's will, read books about the Orient, prayed, and in 1873 announced their decision to leave the school and go as missionaries to China. Lottie's younger sister, Edmonia, had gone to China under Southern Baptist sponsorship the year before at the youthful age of twenty-one.[4]

In September 1873, Charlotte Digges Moon set out from San Francisco on the way to China and a work which would consume the rest of her life. In October she arrived at the Southern Baptist North China Mission in Tengchow, joining that group of first generation missionaries sent out before the Civil War. These "old hands," twenty-year veterans, had little strategy for easing newcomers into the work. They simply sent them into ministry and expected the novices to sink or swim. Lottie swam; her sister Edmonia did not fare so well. Young and immature, "Eddie" had experienced tremendous culture shock and responded with what the other missionaries judged to be foolishness and hysteria. She had become chronically ill and received little sympathy from veterans at the mission.

Lottie tried to help but her contrasting energy and rapid adaptation to the hardships magnified her sister's failures. By 1875 Edmonia Moon had returned to America, much to Lottie's sorrow, the relief of the other missionaries, and the sometimes judgmental attitudes of those Southern Baptists who saw her retreat from China as a repudiation of her high calling.[5]

The months after Eddie's departure produced a crisis in Lottie's life, creating doubts about her call and discouragement about her work. The Chinese schoolchildren disappointed her; she was lonely and could do little independent work without the permission of senior, male missionaries. In 1877 she wrote the Foreign Mission Board: "I am especially bored to death living alone. I don't find my own society either agreeable or edifying . . . I really think a few more winters like the one just past will put an end to me. This is no joke, but dead earnest."[6]

In these dark days came an invitation from a former suitor, Crawford Toy, to return to America and become his bride. Then, Toy promised, the two could go together as missionaries to Japan. Lottie considered the offer and accepted. Crawford Toy was a professor at the fledgling Southern Baptist Theological Seminary, then in Greenville, South Carolina, and a biblical scholar of growing repute. However, he was becoming increasingly suspect among Southern Baptists for his "liberal" views on evolution and biblical inspiration. Under fire from the constituents, Toy resigned the seminary and in 1880 became professor of Hebrew and Oriental Languages at Harvard. In the meantime, Lottie had reconsidered her decision regarding marriage, perhaps because she could not share his theological views, but also because she had decided that her destiny was to "go it alone" in China. Years later, when asked if she had ever been in love, she replied, "Yes, but God had first claim on my life, and since the two conflicted, there could be no question about the result."[7] While the doubts often returned, from that time forward Lottie Moon's life was inseparable from her ministry with the people of China. She accepted the difficult tension between her love for the Chinese and the stark realities of life in a foreign land where work was hard, response slow, and conditions dangerous.

The story of that work is far too complex for this brief sermon. Perhaps three different aspects of her ministry will help us to understand something of her approach to missions and her personal qualities as a pioneer woman missionary.

First, Lottie had to learn to work with other missionaries and that in itself required a major portion of God's grace. The Southern Baptist missionaries in nineteenth-century China were a tough lot of seasoned campaigners with definite ideas as to how the gospel was to be preached. Lottie arrived on the heels of a confrontation between T. P. Crawford and J. B. Hartwell, two missionary war-horses, over the use of church property and leadership of the mission. These men, burning with evangelistic zeal for Chinese, were much less compassionate toward one another. Crawford, a crusty controversialist who ultimately separated from the Southern Baptist board, disagreed with Hartwell on everything from the worship services to the use of mission funds. He even suspected that Hartwell was somehow involved in a Chinese plot to murder him.[8]

Lottie soon learned that even missionaries could be petty and egocentric. Caught in the middle, she sought to moderate in the dispute and succeeded in retaining the goodwill of both families. She frequently spoke out against those doctrinal, legal, and personal squabbles which diverted missionaries from their evangelical tasks.

Second, Lottie Moon took the gospel to the Chinese people. There was much to learn—language, dialects, customs, culture, and techniques for working in the good news at every opportunity. Early on she confronted the Chinese contempt and curiosity for foreigners, particularly women who acted in ways beyond their carefully regimented roles. To many she was a "foreign devil," to be suspected and despised. But she worked determinedly teaching women and children, giving rudimentary medical care, and traveling inland with increasing regularity. She wrote home, "I am still a teacher, but my school is movable and my pupils are constantly changing."[9]

In 1885 she traveled fifty miles inland to P'ingtu, becoming the first Southern Baptist woman to begin a new mission outpost in China. This also began a new relationship with the rural Chinese which she treasured throughout her life. As she lived and worked among them, Lottie's attitude toward the Chinese changed significantly.

In her early days in China she maintained distinctly Western style dress, believing that to wear Chinese clothes was to pretend to understand a culture which could never be fully assimilated. She considered the Chinese to be heathens, with a fascinating but distasteful culture. Their life-style, food, and sanitary habits led her to join others in labeling them the "Great Unwashed." With time, however, she became increasingly more Chinese in her own life-style. She wrote that new missionaries

must be men and women of absolute self-consecration, ready to come down and live among the natives, to wear the Chinese dress, and live in Chinese houses, rejoicing in the footsteps of him who "though he was rich, yet for our sakes he became poor." . . . We do not ask people to come out to live in costly foreign style . . . bearly touching the heathen world with the tips of their fingers but we ask them to come prepared to cast their lots with the natives.[10]

And so she did—wearing Chinese clothes, accepting Chinese customs, later rebuking those in China and America who persisted in calling the Chinese heathens. She wrote: "Isn't it time that we missionaries part company with those who roll this word *heathen* under their tongues as a sweet morsel of contempt? Shall we Christians at home or in mission fields be courteous in preaching the gladdest tidings on earth, or not?"[11] Rather, she said, let us "speak respectfully of non-Christian peoples."[12]

Thus Lottie Moon was not afraid to change. Her love was not merely for Christian Chinese but for all Chinese whom she treated with respect, whether they accepted Christ's gospel or not. She did not simply identify herself with the Chinese, in many respects she became one with them.

Third, as she moved closer to the Chinese people, Lottie Moon sought to awaken the consciousness of Southern Baptists to the needs of missions, even when it threatened traditional Baptist practices. She urged Baptist women to unite with missionaries through prayer and fund-raising. Miss Moon was pleased when the Woman's Missionary Union was formed in 1888, but disappointed that Virginia women were prevented from joining due to the opposition of men who felt that such an organization was beyond the women's proper authority in the church.[13] Likewise, she fought for the equality of women missionaries in determining policies on the field. She did not argue with the practice of men teaching men and women teaching women unless there were no male missionaries in areas where Chinese men were hungry for the gospel. When such men came to her inquiring of the faith, she would not turn them away or wait for a male missionary, no matter how much it scandalized the "folks back home." And it did! She wrote of an occasion when a group of men insisted that she teach them of the gospel. She acquiesced saying, "I could not hinder their calling upon me to lead in prayer."[14]

The years rolled by and Lottie Moon grew old in China. There she faced angry mobs, cold, disease, assorted wars, rebellions, and persecution. From America she confronted lack of funds, criticism for instructing men, and even the accusation that she was not teaching correct doctrine.[15] (Lottie Moon a heretic?) She struggled with periods of doubts, depression, fear, and discouragement. She lost most of her teeth, gave away all of her money, and the years of hardship finally affected her state of mind. By 1912 she was given to deep melancholia, convinced that her people in P'ingtu were starving. Determined to die with them, she stopped eating. When the missionaries finally discovered her secret, it was too late. Barely alive, her frail body, all fifty pounds of it, was placed on a ship bound for America. She died four days out of China, on Christmas Eve, 1912. Her ashes were returned to Virginia and the Christmas mission offering she had begun among Southern Baptists years before was given her name.

What does Lottie Moon teach us? A life-time of lessons! Perhaps she reminds us of two important truths which are often overlooked in her sometimes overly romanticized life. She reveals something of the nature of Christian humility and the reality of failure in the pursuit of the gospel.

What kind of humility was it? Not some cringing, fearful quality which kept her from confronting life and human suffering. Lottie Moon spoke out against cruelty, indifference, hunger, and sin. She demanded to be treated as an equal partner with men in the mission endeavor. She made her views known, even in the face of opposition. Nor was hers a pharisaical humility which pointed at the "heathen" Chinese saying, "Lord, I thank you that I am not like those sinners." She would not clothe her own sins in the shabby rags of false humility and common pride. Rather, she, like her Lord, chose to become of no reputation. She humbled herself for the sake of others.

In the second chapter of Philippians, Paul provides us with a magnificent hymn to Christ which gives insight into the nature of humility in its divine and human expressions. In Jesus Christ, Paul writes, we discover the God who humbles himself, the God whose very nature is humility. Jesus Christ—in the form of God—emptied himself—became a servant; humbled himself—became obedient. The God who consistently identifies himself with the lowly and the oppressed, has become one of them. In Christ he laid aside those Godlike qualities—omnipotence, omnipresence, omniscience—to accept the weakness of humanity. God took on human flesh; God humbled himself, even to death on a cross. It was no game, no trick. He did not pretend to suffer, to agonize, or die. Jesus Christ lost himself for the sins of the world. He came among us as one with no reputation.

Scandalous behavior: associating with sinners.

Scandalous teaching: loving his enemies.

Scandalous and humiliating death on a criminal's cross.

And still his words haunt us: "When you save your life, you lose it. When you lose your life for my sake and the gospel's, you find it."

As God humbles himself, so he calls us to a life of humility. Lottie Moon discovered that truth and so must we. If we are to follow Christ, we must discover the liberating humility of his life. It is not that we, in ourselves, do something which makes us humble. Rather we are changed at the foundation of our lives. We move from obsession with ourselves to concern for God and others. We accept the fact that at the center of life we experience a basic trust in God, the God who humbles himself. Thus humility is a happening rather than an achievement, a gift rather than a reward.

As we humble ourselves, as we become of no reputation, we discover our real worth as persons. It is not a worth secured at the expense of others but the worth of a new, whole person who lives in the light of God's grace, acceptance, and love. Thus to be worth something, to be secure, we do not have to win in every situation. We do not have to look good or be absolutely sure of ourselves to be ourselves. My proficiency, my authority, is not bought at the expense of others. Humility for the individual and the church means that there is no "pecking order," only community and servanthood.

Lottie Moon practiced this humility long after she had become a most famous and admired missionary. On one occasion, after a dispute with a younger colleague, Miss Moon returned to offer her profound apology. The novice protested, "Miss Moon, don't apologize to me. I am so much younger." "Why not?" Lottie answered. "I erred in judgment. You were right and I was wrong, yet I insisted, and you followed my advice. I want you to rescind the action and let the whole [mission] family know it was my doing, not yours."[16] Even as a famous missionary, Lottie Moon knew what it was to be of no reputation for the sake of Christian charity and community. So you and I must seek to learn humility in a world which too often rewards pride, self-conceit, and power.

Lottie Moon and the Word of God which came to her teach us something else. When we become of no reputation for the sake of the gospel, our understanding of success and failure changes radically. Lottie Moon's life brings prophetic condemnation upon the obsession with statistical and programmatic success rampant among many American evangelicals, particularly Southern Baptists. While Miss Moon's life is lauded by Baptists as a spiritual success, statistically her "convert/baptism" rate leaves something to be desired. Frequently she went into areas where she was ridiculed and cursed as a "white devil." More often than not her words were ignored by the populace, interested in this strange foreigner but indifferent to her message. Nonetheless she was determined to give herself, to live and work, trusting God to supply the results. The work would be slow, with results secured in God's own good time. She wrote: "The missionary's first object is to convince them [the Chinese] that he is human and that he is their sincere friend. By patience and gentleness and unwearied love, he wins upon them until there begins to be a diversion in sentiment."[17] That kind of tedious work often produced more immediate failure than success.

At P'ingtu her initial efforts indeed seemed less than successful. One scholar writes:

A logical restructuring of events indicates that she had indeed miscalculated in P'ingtu at virtually every turn. Her leavening evoked no conversions in the city, and her austere life did not strike her neighbors as identical with their own. Her success at Sha-ling was due not to woman's work but to local males with previous religious interest. . . . As an honest person, which Lottie Moon seems clearly to have been, she could not have emerged feeling like a very good leader.[18]

Whether one agrees completely with that evaluation or not, it is clear that Lottie Moon had learned to live with failure. It was surely painful for her, but she had decided that she would share the gospel and be faithful whether anyone believed or not, trusting God to "give the increase."

To hear Paul tell it, the gospel for the people "of no reputation" is apt to produce just that kind of life. Throughout his letters, he recounts the difficulties, yes, even the failures, which came to him as he preached the gospel. His preaching of the good news had produced hardship, pain, inconvenience, and conflict. It has succeeded, but on terms very different from those with which the world judges success.

And that is horrible news for many of us. In our Baptist context we have often stressed success for ourselves and our churches as if Christianity were nothing but a succession of triumphs. But we run from any hint of weakness or failure. Success becomes the primary aim of the church, success determined by a particular set of criteria: larger crowds, bigger buildings, elaborate programs, expanded budgets. Life, particularly gospel life, does not require us to win, it requires us to grow and to be faithful to God. The church which succeeds with all the right programs, numbers, and fanfares but at the neglect of humility and servanthood will find hollow victory in its achievements.

In success or failure, you and I and all the church have but one gospel: Christ crucified. We proclaim that word in all its far-reaching implications and if we are a success, that is good. But if we are failures to the world, that is all right, too. We are called not to triumph but to truth. Thus winning comes from God and is defined on his terms.

The experiences of Paul and Lottie Moon are indeed good news for those whom we often label as losers—churches struggling to proclaim the gospel in hostile environments; preachers who work where there is little outward success but tremendous human need; Christians who serve God quietly for a lifetime and receive little appreciation from the church or the world; and those who plant the seed but have no immediate response and are often judged as failures along the way. The gospel is for all of us, for every one of us is a loser sooner or later.

So it is all right to fail. It is painful, but it is all right. In fact, failure at some point is inevitable. When we become a people of no reputation, we accept the fact of the spiritual life that sometimes when you minister as best you can, when you give ministry your best shot, you fail. Yet somehow, God is the kind of God who is at his best in our weakness, our failure, our lack of repute. It is in those persons who like Jesus become of no reputation, humble themselves, become servants that God has chosen to reveal himself. Failure is pain; it is humiliation. But through it all there is the grace of God. "My grace is made perfect in weakness," so the Word of God came to Paul, to Lottie, and to each one of us.

Let us together confess what we really are, a people of no reputation, given to frustration, even failure, that the gospel of Jesus Christ may be proclaimed to all the world.

Think of it, the good news of Jesus Christ made known in China by a tiny, practically toothless woman who starved herself to death—how disgusting! Hallelujah!

Notes

1. Irwin T. Hyatt, Jr., *Our Ordered Lives Confess* (Cambridge, Mass.: Harvard University Press, 1976), p. 94.

2. Ibid, pp. 94-95.

3. Ibid., p. 95.

4. Ibid., p. 96.

5. Catherine B. Allen, *The New Lottie Moon Story* (Nashville: Broadman Press, 1980), pp. 111-12.

6. Hyatt, p. 98.

7. Ibid., p. 99.

8. Allen, pp. 104-106.

9. Ibid., p. 151.

10. Ibid., p. 174.

11. Ibid., p. 201.

12. Ibid., p. 202.

13. Ibid., p. 174.
14. Ibid., p. 179.
15. Ibid., p. 245.
16. Ibid., p. 215.
17. Ibid., p. 173.
18. Hyatt, pp. 117-18.

Selected Bibliography

ALLEN, CATHERINE B. *The New Lottie Moon Story.* Nashville: Broadman Press, 1980.

BEAVER, R. PIERCE. *All Loves Excelling.* Grand Rapids: Eerdmans Publishing Co., 1968.

HUNT, ALMA, and ALLEN, CATHERINE B. *History of the Woman's Missionary Union.* Revised edition. Nashville: Convention Press, 1976.

HYATT, IRWIN T. JR. *Our Ordered Lives Confess, Three Nineteenth-Century American Missionaries in East Shantung.* Cambridge, Massachusetts: Harvard University Press, 1976.

LAWRENCE, UNA ROBERTS. *Lottie Moon.* Nashville: Sunday School Board of the Southern Baptist Convention, 1927.

10.
Across the Ages and in the Pulpit

In September 1980, I sat in the dining hall of Yale Divinity School and listened as the redoubtable Roland Bainton charmed his way into the hearts of another generation of seminary students. On that evening he traced the history of Yale through the lives of some of its most famous faculty and students, among them Jonathan Edwards, David Brainerd, Timothy Dwight, and Nathaniel William Taylor.

The evening was hot and muggy, the room crowded and stuffy but Bainton held us spellbound for ninety minutes, much longer than the average sermon and much better than the average lecture. Along with stories, humorous and reverent, Bainton, a sage among church historians, said two things which were particularly intriguing to me. First, he insisted quite vehemently that the historian is not merely a peddler of facts, names, and dates. "You can't write history without passion," he adamantly proclaimed. And of course he was right. There is no real accounting of the great events of human experience which can avoid some emotional involvement in the defeats and victories, debates and compromises which helped to create them. History is not merely a dead and dusty record, it lives again as we retell the stories and experience similar struggles in our own day.

Second, Bainton, the "passionate" historian, did something else. He told a multitude of stories about Americans who preached the Scriptures, fought slavery, debated doctrine, and worked for social justice; then he turned to more ancient words from the book of Hebrews. "And now seeing we are surrounded by so great a cloud of witnesses, let us run with patience the race that is set before us, looking unto Jesus, the author and the finisher of our faith." With that text he reminded us that we, like some colonial Americans and some early

Christian martyrs, belonged to a people, the people of God. In that brief verse, Scripture and history, past and present, became one. Somehow the faith and deeds of those witnesses had meaning for our own faith and life. We had a heritage. We were a part of a community. We *remembered* who we *are!*

That is really what this little volume is about. It says that we cannot view the life of the church with distant objectivity and without some passion for the great ideas, the foolish mistakes, and the unending debates which have confronted the people of God in every age. It is an effort to show that the contemporary church cannot leap over two thousand years of history from the New Testament to the present, ignoring those events which have occurred along the way. It suggests that the way in which the Word of God comes to other persons in other times is important to us and our own confrontations with that Word and with one another.

This is not a book of preaching on church history. The materials recorded here are not "talks" or lectures, they are sermons aimed at proclaiming the truth of Scripture within the framework of historical event. They represent one type of sermon which might be used, not as a steady diet, but as a periodic tool for relating Scriptures and history to contemporary questions and controversies. They are historical narratives which inform biblical admonitions and current issues in the church and the world.

Not everyone will choose to utilize such an approach in the pulpit but that is less significant than the recognition of the need to awaken a greater historical consciousness in the preacher and the congregation. If other methods for meeting those ends may be developed, all the better. If historical materials are ignored, misused, or utilized only as an occasional sermon illustration, the church's sense of identity will be more difficult to discover.

There are many benefits to be gained from this type of sermon presentation both for the preacher and the congregation. In general, it provides needed variety in preaching. Truth is, many worship services are characterized by a Sunday to Sunday sermonic sameness which becomes all too predictable for those who attend church regularly. The old "three points and a poem" approach may not be the norm, but the basic plan of explanation, illustration, application, and conclusion may be united with repetitious themes to produce sermons which listeners anticipate, hear with limited attention, or greet with yawns of indifference. Preachers themselves may grow negligent in their sermon preparation, casual in their approach, or seek to compensate for problems of content with sensational tactics and flamboyant delivery.

Sermon series such as this one provide the minister with new opportunities for research, new subject matter for investigation, and a varied approach to sermon presentation. They also give the minister an occasion to fulfill various roles as teacher, historian, and preacher.

First, the use of historical narrative in the sermon enables the preacher to exercise the role of teacher in the church. From the biblical perspective this task is important to the work of the pastor. Paul writes that some are called to be pastor-teachers, offering the church the gifts of both *kerygma* and *didache,* proclamation and teaching (Eph. 4:11-12).

Sermons utilizing extensive historical materials offer the preacher an excellent chance to impart knowledge, raise issues, and present new insights within the context of biblical proclamation. Few, for example, have even heard of Sojourner Truth, let alone become familiar with the details of her fascinating life. Even a brief introduction to her life raises issues relating to slavery, civil rights, Christian freedom, the role of women, and religious experience. Perhaps church members will be challenged to do further reading regarding persons and movements discussed from the pulpit.

As teacher, the preacher imparts new information which exposes certain caricatures and preconceived notions about various groups and individuals in Christian history. Stereotypes regarding other traditions abound in the church. Sometimes the pulpit has been a place which fostered prejudices as preachers misused history or foisted their own preconceived but uninformed notions on their listeners. Such questions as, "Do Catholics really preach the gospel?" "Do Quakers believe in the Bible?" "Was Martin Luther a victim of alcohol, lust, or unresolved conflict with his father?" and "Did John Wesley really believe a Christian could achieve complete perfection in this life?" are among many of the common inquiries made about the great leaders of Christian history.

The sermons in this volume may not answer all these and related questions, but they nonetheless provide a context for better understanding these leaders and their movements beyond the glib generalization or the casual caricature. Such sermons also allow the preacher to correct those caricatures often associated with strange or unfamiliar traditions.

The use of history in the teaching office of the preacher permits him/her to trace the development of doctrines and practices beyond the biblical period. Communion and baptismal observances, outstanding doctrines, and denominational development may also be examined.

One other word about this aspect of the minister's task might be suggested. In an increasingly secular context where many people do not receive basic religious instruction in Sunday school, catechism classes, or in other teaching agencies of the church, ministers can no longer assume (if they ever could) that their listeners have knowledge of the rudiments of Christian faith and history. The teaching role of the preacher thus becomes extremely important as a means of informing those whose only consistent participation in the church is through the Sunday morning service of worship.

Second, historical emphases in sermons permit the preacher to serve as the historian-in-residence for the congregation, a task important for the intellectual development of the minister as well as the spiritual edification of the church. Here the preacher becomes, not just the dispenser of facts, but the interpreter of events. In ancient times and in many tribal contexts today, every community had its historian. These persons told and retold the stories of a people to new generations, helping to provide an identity and a sense of heritage. Much of it was oral history, passed on verbally long before, if ever, it was written down. In a sense the preacher as historian proclaims orally the heritage of a people as local comminity, as denomination and as spiritual communion, the community of faith. This is a role which modern ministers must cultivate and take seriously.

In some Christian communities the sense of history is often rejected, ignored, or dismissed as irrelevant. Many contemporary Christians prefer to move immediately from the New Testament to the present, as if little of importance has occurred along the way. Some sectarian groups repudiate much of Christian history as a corruption of the true teachings of the New Testament church by assorted enemies—Catholics, Protestants, secularists, politicians, or selected denominations. They denounce "man-made tradition" as harmful to true biblical Christianity and found their doctrines "only on the Bible" uncorrupted by the mistakes of the past. Others in their concern to be relevant ignore the past as inadequate for the pressing problems of the modern situation.

As historian, the preacher shows that history is important and acknowledges that every group has a tradition, recognized or not. Those who fail to explore their heritage will often develop a "traditionless tradition" in which the pragmatic actions of the moment become the dogmas of the future, frequently uninformed by the Scripture or the past.

The preacher as historian evaluates the current state of the church and the world by tracing in the present those themes which reoccur throughout Christian history. James White notes that preaching is not merely imparting new knowledge but also repeating those truths which the church has heard before but has neglected or forgotten. It is "a rediscovery of the salvation events which we already know—and constantly forget."[1]

In the sermons presented here, and others like them, the preacher examines issues of peace and perfection, faith and grace, community and freedom as they have been confronted by other believers in other times. We discover that sometimes the response made by Francis, Wesley, or Sojourner Truth to the questions of their day fail to relate to modern problems, but their mistakes inform our own efforts and surely their faith strengthens ours.

Often in a series such as this, however, the minister may show that many problems of the church recur throughout Christian history. Indeed, the historian/preacher insists that the church can never be truly objective in its interpretation of the Scripture, the past or the present. It is always in the world and bound to the culture in one way or another.

As historian, the preacher also affirms the value of heritage for every Christian community. In some historical sermons the preacher/ historian stresses those common "roots" shared with many individuals and movements of the past, discovering common unity in Christ with Catholics, Quakers, Baptists, Methodists, and yes, even an occasional Shaker. Other sermons distinguish one tradition from another, describing the differences and distinctions in church, sect, and denomination. The medieval monk, the heartwarmed Anglican, the celibate Shaker, and the slave mystic may share a common spirit, but their context, their doctrines, and their life-styles are drastically different. Such differences should not be minimized but honestly acknowledged and carefully examined. These sermons remind the listener that while similarities exist and differences abound there is nonetheless a heritage of faith which informs the present. The preacher as historian helps the church, local or at large, to have a sense of identity, to have a past as well as a present and a future.

Finally, along with the historical emphasis in sermons, the minister must continue to be preacher. That may be the most challenging aspect in the preparation of this type of sermon. For in this experience the preacher must balance historical detail with biblical imperative and contemporary relevance.

Too much history turns the sermon into a lecture which may lose the attention of the listeners in the complexities of historical method. Too little Bible keeps the sermon from becoming the proclamation of the good news, a timeless event beyond all historical periods. Too little application makes the sermon a "nice talk" about the past with limited significance for the present. Thus the preacher struggles to keep all these factors in balance. This means that such sermons require time in preparation, perhaps more time than the usual sermon because extensive research and careful writing are required. Every element of the sermon—historical material, biblical proclamation, contemporary significance—must be woven into a narrative which tells the "whole story" in twenty to twenty-five minutes. Too much detail becomes difficult to follow, while too little detail leads to generalization and overstatement, thereby defeating a major purpose of the series.

That is why such a series is of value to the minister as preacher. It offers a challenge to the preacher as communicator and proclaimer of the Word of God while expanding research skills and pulpit gifts. Most of all, it allows the preacher to exercise the prophetic dimension of preaching from the perspective of Scripture and history. Perhaps a word of "thus *saith* the Lord" in the present is more clearly proclaimed as one also struggles with the issue of "thus *said* the Lord" in other times and other cultures. The preacher may better come to grips with his or her prophetic role by studying the true and false prophets of the past.

In writing these sermons the preacher must struggle with words—how to communicate old and new ideas clearly and concisely—and that is another of the valuable lessons which a series such as this provides. The preacher is storyteller; the preacher is communicator. The demands of these sermons for a balance of history, Scripture, and contemporary relevance require that careful attention be given to the use of words and the structure of sentences. While this is true of every sermon which the preacher prepares, a new approach and a different type of material offers the chance to develop new skills in word usage and sentence structure. That challenge, often neglected by the preacher, may become one of the most exciting aspects of the preparation of sermons.

A sermon series of this nature is a lot of work. It will receive mixed reviews from those who desire "real preaching," not all that "history stuff." Others, however, will hear it as a fresh word from God. It will put some people to sleep (as do all sermons, ultimately) but some will be challenged to reflect on the gospel in new ways. Hopefully, it will encourage preachers to say again what they believe and what they do not. Perhaps it will even make us more captive to the Word of God and more committed to our calling as ministers in that community of forgiven and forgiving sinners, the church of Jesus Christ.

The Preparation of Historical Sermons:
Some Basic Suggestions

The following comments represent basic procedures for developing biblical sermons from historical materials.

1. Plan the series well in advance. It is not something which can be developed overnight. It requires time for research and writing as well as for advance publicity and congregational preparation. Allow at least four to six months of preparation.

2. Select the individuals or movements you wish to examine. You may decide to establish a basic theme which appears in each of the sermons or you may choose topics which allow you to deal with a broad range of issues such as worship, peace, salvation, or sanctification.

3. Do not hesitate to select persons and groups who hold different beliefs from your own. Choose those with whom you disagree but do not use them as whipping boys (or girls) to prove that your own views are more correct. Try to discover those positive, biblical concepts which they were trying to elucidate. Do not hesitate to critique their weaknesses but concentrate primarily on the positive lessons which they teach about the gospel. If you cannot find such contributions in certain persons, select other persons or groups. Acknowledge disagreement but search for common biblical truth.

4. Develop a brief bibliography on each topic. Do not attempt to

read everything available. Avoid studies which may be too technical. When dealing with persons, try to find "primary" source materials, journals, diaries, treatises, autobiographies, and other books written by the individuals themselves. Parallel these sources by reading one or two good biographies. Articles or other brief materials may provide succinct overviews which will help efforts at limiting material. Be careful to make good notes and thorough documentation. You may find many materials which can be used in other types of sermons.

5. Select a Scripture text for each topic. If at all possible, choose a text to which the subjects appealed in their efforts to call others to the faith. Most of the time you will find such Scriptures easily. If not, choose one which you believe applies to your subject. Develop your own exegesis of the text and determine whether or not the persons or groups you are discussing were true to the text. Do not merely read the Scripture and then preach without reference to it, expecting the listeners to make the necessary connections. Weave the text into the narrative of your sermon as it relates to both the past and the present. Try to show the way in which persons discussed in your sermon were themselves confronted by the Word of God and how that same Word comes to us today. It may be helpful as a rule of thumb to divide the sermon material roughly into one-third narrative, one-third biblical material, and one-third application. That is only a general guide and each sermon will vary.

6. When writing the sermon, the following guidelines might be used.

(1) Use a manuscript for this type of sermon. Even if you do not use it in the pulpit, you need a narrative which flows clearly and which incorporates the necessary facts into crisp phrases and simple style. If you become too technical or complex, you will often lose your audience and turn the sermon into a lecture.

(2) Use quotations sparingly and selectively, for emphasis only. Avoid lengthy quotations which are difficult for the audience to follow.

(3) Avoid sentimentalizing or romanticizing your subjects as "super" Christians. Show their frailties as well as their strengths. Do not succumb to the temptation to generalize in suggesting that modern Christianity would solve all its problems by returning to the methods of the past.

(4) Do not make the sermons too long. If you go beyond twenty to twenty-five minutes, you will lose many in your audience no matter

how fascinating the material seems. Save some of the extra illustrations and ideas for later sermons.

(5) The series should extend no longer than four to six weeks. If it goes too long, the people will tire of this approach. If it is interesting enough and brief enough, they may ask you to do it again later on.

(6) Schedule the series at a time of particular emphasis in the church. I first preached the sermons in this book during the summer when there were few special observances in the Christian calendar and when interest in church often wanes. Certain topics might be used during Lent or during the month of October in preparation for Reformation Sunday. Another series might deal with local heritage as preparation for observing a special date in the life of a specific congregation — homecoming, anniversary, or centennial.

7. Organize the entire service around the theme of your sermon. When preaching on Martin Luther, for example, no one should fail to include "A Mighty Fortress Is Our God" among the congregational hymns. Wesleyan hymns can be used when dealing with John Wesley, and Black spirituals are appropriate when discussing Sojourner Truth or other figures of Afro-American history.

8. Finally, allow these individuals and their pilgrimages to speak to you as a Christian minister. Identify with their struggles and communicate that to your congregation. Their frailties will give you courage and their victories will give you strength. As you prepare such a series you may even discover that the church is bigger than you ever imagined, made up of some of the most unexpected persons who accomplished great things in Christ's name, often in very unorthodox ways. The Spirit, like the wind, blows where it will, making itself known in a wide variety of persons and traditions. And, as the early Christians confessed, "where the Spirit of the Lord is, there is the one true Church, apostolic and universal."

Note

1. James White, *New Forms of Worship* (Nashville: Abingdon Press, 1971), p. 41.